# FREEDOM RAILWAY

## CHINA AND THE TANZANIA-ZAMBIA LINK

# FREEDOM RAILWAY

## CHINA AND THE TANZANIA-ZAMBIA LINK

### MARTIN BAILEY

LONDON
**REX COLLINGS**
1976

First published in Great Britain by
Rex Collings Ltd,
69 Marylebone High Street, London W1

ISBN 0860 36 0245

Typesetting by Malvern Typesetting Services
Printed and bound in Great Britain by
Billing & Sons Limited
Guildford, London and Worcester

# CONTENTS

# ABBREVIATIONS

| | |
|---|---|
| ANC | African National Congress of Zambia |
| COREMO | Revolutionary Committee for Mozambique |
| EAR | East African Railways |
| FAO | Food and Agriculture Organization |
| FRELIMO | Front for the Liberation of Mozambique |
| IDZ | Intensive Development Zone |
| MPLA | Popular Movement for the Liberation of Angola |
| OAU | Organization of African Unity |
| RR | Rhodesia Railways |
| TANU | Tanganyika African National Union |
| TAZARA | Tanzania-Zambia Railway Authority |
| UDI | Unilateral Declaration of Independence |
| UNIP | United National Independence Party of Zambia |
| UNITA | National Union for the Total Independence of Angola |
| ZANU | Zimbabwe African National Union |
| ZAPU | Zimbabwe African People's Union |
| ZR | Zambia Railways |

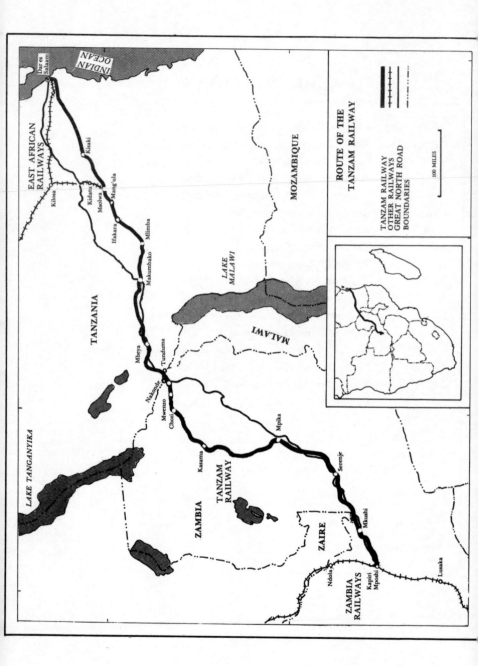

ROUTE OF THE
TANZAM RAILWAY

TANZAM RAILWAY
OTHER RAILWAYS
GREAT NORTH ROAD
BOUNDARIES

100 MILES

# ZAMBIA'S RAIL OUTLETS TO THE SEA

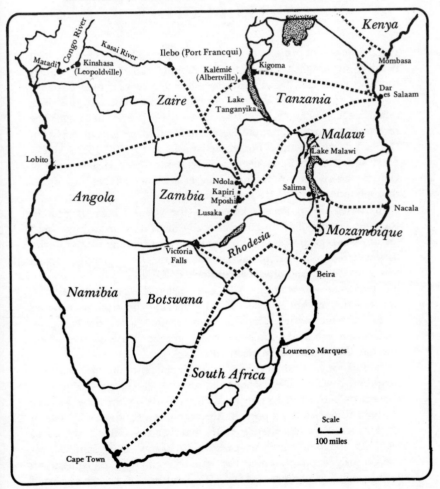

# INTRODUCTION

Few development projects in Africa have been so highly charged with political dynamite as the Tanzania-Zambia railway. Cecil Rhodes first conceived the line almost a century ago as part of a Cape-to-Cairo railway that would slice open the African continent to British imperial rule. The transcontinental link was never built and the section between the Zambian Copperbelt and the Tanzanian port of Dar es Salaam remained uncompleted until the end of 1975. Almost 1,200 miles of gleaming steel track have now been laid—thanks to Chinese assistance—providing Zambia with a reliable rail outlet through independent Africa to the sea.

In Africa the project is known as the Great Uhuru (Freedom) Railway—rather than by the politically neutral 'Tanzam' tag—and the line was regarded as essential for two major reasons, one strategic, the other economic. First of all an outlet through independent Africa was a strategic necessity for landlocked Zambia. When Zambian independence was won on 24 October 1964, the country's southern border—the mighty Zambezi River—became the frontier between black and white Africa. To the south lay regimes where the European settlers were grimly determined to hang on to their privileged position and halt the advance of majority rule.

Zambia was born economically dependent on its southern neighbour, white-ruled Rhodesia, and all its foreign trade was carried over the rail bridge at Victoria Falls on the long journey through Rhodesia to seaports in Mozambique. Rhodesia's Unilateral Declaration of Independence (UDI), barely a year after Zambia had won its independence, exacerbated tensions and Zambia was dangerously exposed. Since the country remained dependent on hostile regimes in Southern Africa, a rail outlet to the north appeared essential to preserve the new nation's freedom. The wisdom of embarking on the long link to Dar es Salaam was confirmed on the morning of 9 January 1973 when the Rhodesian regime lowered the barriers across the Victoria Falls Bridge, on the grounds that guerrilla fighters in Rhodesia were operating from Zambian bases, cutting Zambia's outlet to the sea. The Zambian government—in the knowledge that the track of the Tanzam railway would soon be entering Zambia—was able to resist Rhodesian pressure and break the stranglehold of the white South.

In the long term the strategic reasons for the construction of the Tanzam railway may well become less pressing. But there remain strong economic arguments for a rail link between Dar es Salaam and the Copperbelt. The area served by the new line had been badly neglected during the colonial period because of the lack of transport facilities. Pushing a railway through these remote areas, it was hoped, would open up important mineral deposits and rich agricultural lands.

During the colonial era there had been little contact between Tanzania and Zambia. The only overland route was the grandly-titled Great North Road, almost 1,200 miles of dirt track which became an impassable quagmire of mud during the rainy season. Consequently there was little trade between the two countries and, with the new leaders' commitment to African unity, improved transport links appeared essential. Since the economies of African states were orientated towards trade with Europe, the establishment of ties between neighbouring countries was an important element in the search for a more genuine form of independence.

The Tanzam project first hit the headlines of the world press in 1965 with the announcement that the Chinese had offered to finance and build the railway. Requests for assistance had initially been submitted to a number of Western sources—including Britain, the United States, West Germany, France, and the World Bank—as well as to the Soviet Union. But the West, which saw little need for Zambia to break away from its dependence on Southern Africa, was reluctant to put such a large sum of money into a single development project. Already the scene was set for China to embark on its most ambitious move into Africa.

When the call to the West went unanswered, the Tanzanian and Zambian governments resolved to accept the Chinese offer. In November 1967 the initial agreement was signed in Peking and, following a full survey of the route, actual construction began two and a half years later. The Western press, the Tanzanians and Zambians complain, has paid too much attention to the motives of the Chinese and has not concentrated sufficiently on the importance of the railway for the two African countries.

The Tanzam line is the third largest development scheme ever undertaken in Africa, after the Aswan and Volta Dams, as well as being the most important Chinese project in the Third World. China committed a loan of £166 million for the railway, a huge sum for a developing country to provide, which demonstrated the importance that Peking attached to the project. An examination of China's growing relationship with Tanzania and Zambia is also important in showing the co-operative role of the Chinese, rather than the conflict posture that was often, quite unfairly, attributed to Peking's foreign policy.

Over the last decade there has been increasing disillusionment with Western and Soviet aid — among both recipients and donors — along with greater interest in Chinese assistance. Little, however, has been published on how Chinese aid has worked in practice, so the story of the construction of the Tanzam railway provides an important case study of an alternative form of external assistance.

The completion of the Tanzam railway was perceived in very different ways. To the Western powers, angry that the Chinese had entered territory which they considered their own preserve, it was a Red Railway to thrust communism into the very heart of Africa. For the white regimes of Southern Africa, grimly attempting to hold back demands for majority rule, it was seen as Africa's Ho Chi-Minh Trail carrying guerrilla fighters — armed with Chinese thoughts and weapons — to the bank of the Zambezi River. The Chinese regarded the project as a Friendship Route to strengthen the new African states against the forces of imperialism. For the Tanzanians and Zambians it is the Great Uhuru Railway, which should prove an important instrument in increasing their independence.

The Tanzam railway has been shrouded in secrecy. The Chinese, for commendable reasons, have adopted a low profile and have been reluctant to divulge information on what they are careful to describe as a Tanzanian and Zambian railway. Officials from the two African states have been almost as secretive. This is partly because the minority regimes of Southern Africa, who have been strongly opposed to the project, might well attempt to sabotage the line. There has also been so much hostile reporting of the railway in the Western press that the Tanzanian and Zambian authorities have discouraged any foreign journalists from investigating the project.

This book represents an attempt to straighten the record and provide an account of what has been the most important development project undertaken in black Africa since independence. It is much

1 *Victoria Falls Bridge. 'I should like the spray', Cecil Rhodes once said, 'to dash against the railway carriages.' From its completion in 1906 until the closure of the Rhodesian-Zambian border, in 1973, most of Zambia's foreign trade passed over the bridge to ports in Mozambique.*

Acknowledgements
1. Zambia Railways.
2. Nchanga Consolidated Copper Mines.
4, 5, 6 & 7. Zambia Information Services.

2  *Loading copper wire bars. Copper represents 95% of Zambia's exports.*

3  *A forged photograph purporting to be an official Chinese picture— but probably forged by the CIA. The poster asks for volunteers to build the Tanzam railway. Those who wished 'to settle in Africa after the said task is completed will receive good land.' This was almost certainly a crude CIA attempt to stir up anti-Chinese sentiments in Tanzania and Zambia.*

*President Nyerere laying the foundation stone of the Tanzam railway on 28 October 1970 at the Zambian terminal of Kapiri Mposhi.*

*Nyerere and Kaunda touching the first length of track to be laid in Zambia on 27 August 1973.*

6  *The first Tanzam train to enter Zambia.*

7  *Manufacturing spare parts at Chozi workshop. The Chinese placed great emphasis on the need to train Tanzanian and Zambian workers in order that they should be able to maintain the railway once it is in operation.*

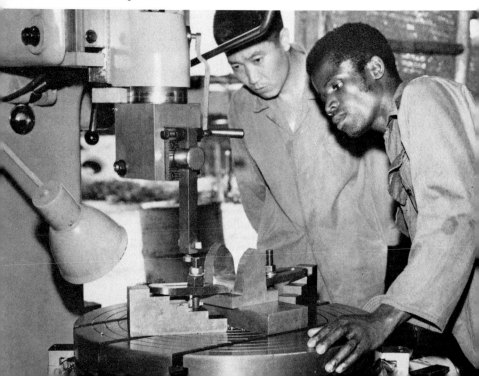

more than simply the story of a railway line. It is a highly political saga that symbolizes and reflects the developments taking place in the Africa of today.

Much of the material was obtained during visits to Tanzania, Zambia, and China. My thanks go out to two trusts, the Barrow Cadbury Fund and the Friends Service Council Work and Study Bursary Fund, for helping to finance my trip to Africa. I should also like to thank all the Tanzanians and Zambians who helped me to understand the significance of the Tanzam railway and who assisted me in various ways during my travels. In particular, I would like to single out Vernon Mwaanga, former Zambian Foreign Minister, who was particularly helpful at the time when his country was busy celebrating the tenth anniversary of independence. Finally I must express my appreciation to two people—Onelia Cardettini and Sydney Bailey—who helped me at all stages of this book.

January 1976

# I

# IMPERIAL DREAM

Cecil Rhodes stood before a large map hanging on the wall and placed his hand over the vast area between South Africa and East Africa. 'I want to see all that red,' he proclaimed, and, he added, what was really needed to open up the African continent was a Cape-to-Cairo railway running through a chain of British colonies.[1] Rhodes had in mind the cartographical red that coloured the atlas, rather than the ideological red of the Chinese railway builders who actually completed the longest remaining section of the imperialist's greatest dream.

In order to grasp the significance of the Tanzam railway, built by Tanzania and Zambia to increase their independence, it is important to examine the role which railways played in opening up the two countries during the colonial era. A glance at the past—at the imperial dream of a Cape-to-Cairo railway and the actual development of rail systems in Tanzania and Zambia—puts the story of the Tanzam line into perspective and makes it easier to understand why Presidents Nyerere and Kaunda were so determined to build a rail link from Dar es Salaam to the Copperbelt.

## BEYOND THE FALLS

'Cape-to-Cairo'! The expression had a magical ring for the Victorians. It conveyed the feeling of power, both physical and spiritual, that led them on to conquer Africa. Sir Edwin Arnold, an editor on the London *Daily Telegraph*, is said to have coined the phrase in 1876. But it was left to Cecil Rhodes to transform the imperial dream into thousands of miles of track. The Cape-to-Cairo line, Rhodes claimed, would 'cut Africa through the centre': civilization—Christianity and trade—would be brought to the Dark Continent.[2] Britain, in return, would gain a string of colonies to provide valuable raw materials and an expanding market for manufactured goods.

The first few miles of track were laid from Cape Town in 1859. Slowly at first, the line was gradually pushed forward and by 1894, with Rhodes' efforts, the railway reached Mafeking. Onwards it went, through Bechuanaland Protectorate and into Southern Rhodesia, to arrive at Bulawayo in 1897. Originally it had been intended to continue the line to Gwelo, cross the Zambezi River at the Kariba Gorge, pass up the Luangwa Valley of Northern Rhodesia, and finally reach the borders of German East Africa. But the outbreak of the Boer War in September 1899, which prevented construction material from reaching Bulawayo, led to a change of plan. Engineering costs would be high and coal deposits at Kariba were found to be of low quality. Instead it was decided to bridge the Zambezi at Victoria Falls.

'I should like the spray', Cecil Rhodes once said, 'to dash against the railway carriages.'[3] An easier bridging point would have been six miles upstream from the Victoria Falls. But the Cape-to-Cairo railway — in homage to Rhodes — crossed the swirling waters of the Zambezi River just 400 yards downstream from the Falls and for five months of the year the latticed steelwork of the bridge is half hidden in spray. Up to 120 million gallons of water pour over the mile-wide ledge of the Falls every minute, dropping 300 feet into the gorge below to send up clouds of spray visible more than twenty miles away. *Mosi-oa-Tunya*, 'the smoke that thunders', is the local name. But when David Livingstone discovered this natural wonder for Europe in 1855 he patriotically renamed the Falls in honour of his monarch.

In 1905, 50 years after Livingstone had first glimpsed the Falls, a railway line was strung over the Zambezi Gorge. The 500-foot arched span of the Victoria Falls Bridge, a design blending perfectly with the grandeur of the scene, provides an awe-inspiring view of the Falls with the rapids of the river 350 feet below. The bridge had been assembled in sections at Darlington in Yorkshire, shipped to Beira, and then transported up the new railway line through Mozambique and Southern Rhodesia. Construction took fourteen months, with the actual erection of the steelwork completed in a mere nine weeks, at a total cost of only £72,000.

Cecil Rhodes had been impatient for the Cape-to-Cairo line to cross Victoria Falls and, as he once remarked, 'there is little satisfaction in knowing the railway will reach there after one's death'.[4] Rhodes had already chosen his burial site, a hill in Southern Rhodesia which he named the View of the World, and from its peak, through a cleft in the distant mountains, there is an unobstructed line of sight on to the northern horizon. It was here, three years before the Zambezi was bridged, that the great imperialist was laid to rest.

Rhodes had never seen the Victoria Falls or visited the lands belonging to his British South Africa Company—and named after him—which lay beyond the Zambezi.

The first train to reach Victoria Falls was gaily decorated with the Union Jack and a plaque inscribed 'We've a long way to go!' The railway, after all, had not been built just to give curious visitors a view of one of the natural wonders of the world: Rhodes expected that the track would be pushed northwards from the Zambezi, probably through East Africa, to the Nile Valley and the Mediterranean.

Back in April 1898 Rhodes had addressed a packed meeting of British South Africa Company shareholders in the City of London to outline a scheme that was characteristically bold: 'I want two million pounds to extend the railway to Lake Tanganyika—about 800 miles . . . you have Kitchener coming down from Khartoum . . . . That gives you Africa—the whole of it . . . .'[5] When Rhodes returned to London early the following year he spent much of his time with Lord Kitchener, Britain's military commander in the Sudan, and together the two men made plans to complete the Cape-to-Cairo project. Rhodes would press northwards, with Kitchener working south through the Sudan, and they would meet in East Africa or the Congo. For Rhodes the problems were political, as well as financial, since his route was blocked by two major European powers. In 1885 the German East Africa Company had taken over all land east of Lake Tanganyika, while in the same year King Leopold II of Belgium annexed the territory to the west of the lake as his personal domain.

One solution was to run the railway to the shore of Lake Tanganyika, using a steamer service northwards. In 1898 Rhodes, on behalf of the British South Africa Company, granted the firm of Tanganyika Concessions rights to 2,000 square miles of mineral resources in Northern Rhodesia and authority to establish a township at the southern end of Lake Tanganyika on the Cape-to-Cairo route. Rhodes also visited Brussels and Berlin the following year to discuss the possibility of routing his Cape-to-Cairo line through Belgian or German territory towards the Nile. But no satisfactory agreements were reached with either King Leopold or the Kaiser.

Victoria Falls never became a stop on a Cape-to-Cairo route and by 1905, when the Zambezi was bridged, the trans-African project had been almost abandoned. Rhodes had died three years earlier and with him went the scheme's most energetic proponent. Political problems of crossing German or Belgian colonial territory appeared insurmountable and the British government was unwilling to finance the line. But the fact that the railway had crossed the Falls was to have an enormous impact on the territory lying north of the Zambezi.

Northern Rhodesia was colonized from the south and this had a profound effect on the country, lasting long after independence was won. In the early 1890s Rhodes and the British South Africa Company had provoked a war between Chief Lobengula and his Matabele subjects. The company then supported the Chief, after forcing him to put his thumbprint to a document giving up all mineral rights on his land, and in 1889 a royal charter was granted to the British South Africa Company (which became known as the Chartered Company) to administer both sides of the Zambezi. The Protectorate of Northern Rhodesia was established in 1911, when North-Eastern and North-Western Rhodesia were amalgamated, and twelve years later the company's rights, with the important exception of mineral royalties, were sold to the British government for £3¾ million.

Work had already begun on the 94-mile railway to Kalomo, the administrative capital of North-Western Rhodesia, even before the completion of the Falls Bridge. A *blondin*, named after a famous tight-rope walker, was strung a thousand feet across the Zambezi Gorge to transport material on an overhead wire and in May 1905, just before the bridge was opened to traffic, the rails reached Kalomo.

Lead and zinc had been discovered in Northern Rhodesia at Broken Hill, named after the rich Australian mine, and this proved a sufficient incentive to continue the railway northwards from Kalomo. Mineral and transport interests interlocked, since the Chartered Company not only controlled Rhodesia Railways, but also received all mining royalties. Without this linkage the line to Broken Hill might well not have been laid and Zambia might have been born with a very different transport pattern.

The 281 miles of track between Kalomo and Broken Hill were laid in a record 277 working days. This section included a 1,400-foot bridge across the Kafue River, the longest in Southern Africa for many years, which was completed in just over five months. Sidings were built every twenty miles or so and at one of these, in an area where lions had proved a particular menace, the only sign of life was the roofs of six huts half a mile away where Lusakaa was the headman. In 1910 a tin shack was erected as a station and fourteen years later the dirt track beside it was named Cairo Road. Lusaka was later to become the capital, with a population now approaching half a million, and Cairo Road, so called because of its position on the trans-African route, has remained one of the few street names to survive the changes of independence.

The last half mile of track into Broken Hill was finished on 11 January 1906 with materials off-loaded from a slowly moving train, carried forward by hand, and laid with such rapidity that the train passed over the newly-laid track without stopping. Lead and zinc ore had been stockpiled at the mine and shipments to Beira, where the ore was sent by sea to a refinery in South Wales, began in September 1906. Eight months later, however, difficulties in the treatment and separation of the ore led to a temporary halt in mining at Broken Hill. Suddenly there was no traffic for the Northern Rhodesian line, and the Cape-to-Cairo railway, then just over 2,000 miles away from Cape Town, languished in the middle of swamp without even a buffer-stop at the terminal.

The extent of Northern Rhodesia's copper deposits was not yet known, so the only hope of generating traffic for the railway was to extend the line into the Congo to tap the mineral wealth of Katanga. Rhodes had tried to secure Katanga for the Chartered Company, although in the end he was foiled by the Belgian king, and by the early 1900s it was clear that that area held considerable copper deposits. Tanganyika Concessions, with its interest in the Belgian company of Union Minière (which mined Katangan copper), wanted a rail link between the Broken Hill and the Elizabethville mines. In 1908 agreement was reached between the Chartered Company and Tanganyika Concessions for the establishment of the Rhodesia-Katanga Junction Railway and Mineral Company to embark on the 132-mile line from Broken Hill to the Congolese border.

With an impressive ceremony the Cape-to-Cairo railway left British territory for the first time on 11 December 1909. A copper spike was used to lay the length of track across the frontier, in homage to the mineral wealth of Central Africa which had benefited the British and Belgian dignitaries present at the event. Ahead there was another 150 miles to the Étoile du Congo mine and when the tracks reached Elizabethville in September 1910 a small mountain of 6,000 tons of copper was waiting for the long journey to the coast. This copper was dispatched south through the Rhodesias to Beira, and then on to Europe, while coal from the Southern Rhodesian mine at Wankie was railed north to the Katangan mines.

The Cape-to-Cairo railway was originally to have passed through East Africa but a series of economic decisions — to tap the Wankie coalfield, cross the Zambezi at the Falls, open up the Broken Hill mine, and secure Katanga's mineral traffic—effectively ended plans to route the line through German East Africa. The first siding after Broken Hill was a collection of huts known as Kapiri Mposhi, meaning Hills of Paradise in the Swaka language, and until the 1960s it was nothing more than a few shacks along the Great North Road. Kapiri Mposhi has since become the terminal of the Tanzam railway, the point where the tracks of Northern Rhodesia's original line meet the new route to Dar es Salaam.

## TANGANYIKA LOOKS SOUTH

While the British South Africa Company had been pushing the Cape-to-Cairo line into Northern Rhodesia, the German East Africa Company had been building its own railways in the territory that was later to become known as Tanganyika. In 1885 Karl Peters had persuaded Germany to declare a protectorate over a large area of East Africa, to be administered by his German East Africa Company, and six years later the German government assumed direct control over the territory.

Work on the territory's first railway, started in 1891, began slowly and only 219 miles of track—inland from the northern port of Tanga—had been laid after twenty years. A more ambitious project, the Central Line running from the capital of Dar es Salam to the port of Kigoma on Lake Tanganyika, was begun in 1907 and opened on the eve of World War I. This 779-mile line was envisaged as a possible rib on the Cape-to-Cairo backbone. Consideration was also given to a branch southwards from the Central Line towards Northern Rhodesia. But when a reconnaissance of this project in 1907 showed that it would have cost the enormous sum of £18 million, the scheme was quickly dropped.

During World War I European rivalries spilled over into East Africa. British forces marched south from Kenya, while troops under the German flag, bravely commanded by General von Lettow-Vorbeck, were pushed towards Northern Rhodesia. After Germany's defeat her overseas empire was placed under the Mandate System of the League of Nations. Ruanda-Urundi, a small but densely populated area in the north-west of German East Africa, fell under Belgian administration.

The rest of German East Africa, known as Tanganyika, was allocated to Britain. Tanganyika—whose name derives from the Swahili expression used to describe the long journey from the coast to

Kigoma — was born. One of the problems which had plagued Rhodes, the difficulty of securing a route for the Cape-to-Cairo line through Belgian or German territory in Africa, had been resolved. With a strip of territories under British control all the way from Cape Town to Cairo — through South Africa, Bechuanaland, Southern and Northern Rhodesia, Tanganyika, Kenya, Uganda, the Sudan, and Egypt — an 'all red' route had become politically feasible.

Soon after the war proposals were revived for a railway to open up the south-west of Tanganyika. The project was championed by European settlers who wanted to establish a string of plantations all the way from South Africa up to Kenya. During the German period European settlers had begun to set up plantations in south-west Tanganyika but, because of transport costs, they tended to concentrate on high-priced, low-bulk, labour-intensive crops such as coffee, tobacco, and tea. By the late 1920s these farmers numbered only 180, partly because of political uncertainties following the change-over from Germany colony to League of Nations territory, but they were a powerful pressure group, urging the colonial administration to consider a railway into south-west Tanganyika. They persuaded the Iringa Provincial Commissioner to write to the Governor in 1925 to explain that a railway would help to erect 'the soundest possible defense against unrest, a contented peasantry'. Originally, the Commissioner had used the word 'communism' in his memo, but this was struck out and replaced by 'unrest'.[6]

In 1925 the East African Commission, consisting of three British MPs, visited Tanganyika and recommended the construction of a railway southwards from the Central Line to Lake Nyasa. This proposal, their report claimed, was one of 'primary importance' for the development of the country, and the Commission's recommendations sparked off a number of preliminary investigations of the project during the late 1920s.[7]

The results of these studies of the railway to the south-west were collected in a report by C. Gillman, Chief Engineer of Tanganyika Railways, which was published in 1929. The most economic route, from Kilosa (on the Central Line) to the eastern shore of Lake Nyasa, and then from the western side of the lake to Broken Hill, would have cost £10 million. Local traffic, however, would have been insufficient to justify the investment. Northern Rhodesia's copper mines were just being opened up on a large scale. It was therefore suggested that if the copper companies could be persuaded to export a significant proportion of their output, possibly around a third of total production, over a new route to Dar es Salaam, the Tanganyikan government should then 'press forward with utmost speed' to build the line.[8] The copper companies, however, were content to continue using the Rhodesian rail route across Victoria Falls and expressed little interest in the proposed line to Dar es Salaam.

Gillman's study was followed a year later by a report on Tanganyika Railways which suggested a direct rail link, avoiding the journey across Lake Nyasa, to the Northern Rhodesian line. This railway, which would have run very close to the actual route that the Tanzam line was to follow 40 years later, would have also cost £10 million. The Great Depression intervened and the proposal was never seriously considered.

After World War II Tanganyika became a UN Trust Territory under British administration. Tanganyika, together with Kenya and Uganda, was already part of an East African common market. Discussions began on the creation of the East Africa High Commission to operate a number of shared services on a joint basis. The most important of these was the railways and on 1 May 1948, with the establishment of the High Commission, the East African Railways and Harbours Administration was formed to take over the lines previously operated by Tanganyika Railways. Once again, as after World War I, European settlers put pressure on the colonial government for a rail link to the south-west of Tanganyika. A preliminary reconnaissance of the project in November 1949 suggested that the line could be justified only if effective steps were taken to develop the areas that would be served by the railway. A full report of the project, presented in June 1952, was based on a thorough investigation of the line. The first part of the study, an engineering survey compiled by East African Railways, showed that the link was 'practical from an engineering standpoint'. Some sections, however, would be difficult and expensive. Total costs of the 1,128 miles from Masimbu, on the Central Line, to the Rhodesian railway at Kapiri Mposhi would be £33 million.[9]

The second part of the study, prepared by the London consultants Sir Alexander Gibb and Partners, assessed the economic potential of the areas which would be served by the line. Traffic, leaving out of account the possible future development of mineral resources from south-west Tanganyika, would be primarily agricultural. Prospects for agricultural development in Northern Rhodesia were poor, because of infertile soils, but two areas in Tanganyika—the Kilombero and Usangu Valleys—showed good promise. The report was careful to stress the importance of food production. 'New evils have arisen, nourished on discontent and starvation, and food has become the principal weapon — perhaps the only weapon — whereby we can permanently defend civilization as we know it in the Western world.'[10] Developments in the areas served by the projected line had not yet, however, created sufficient traffic to support a railway. The crucial assumption made by the Gibb report was that the line would carry no Northern Rhodesian copper because transport costs would be higher than on the existing route to Beira. Nevertheless, the Gibb report remarked, a link between British East Africa and British Central Africa would provide 'considerable benefit from a strategic point of view'.[11]

The negative conclusions of the Gibb study meant that the Tanzam project was never again seriously considered during the colonial period. By the late 1950s it was clear that both Tanganyika and Northern Rhodesia were heading towards independence. The European settler community, which had been the strongest pressure group calling for the line, lost much of its influence. Britain became increasingly concerned to reap quick returns on investment in Africa without tying up capital in the development of long-term infrastructure. Kenya and Uganda, Tanganyika's partners in East African Railways, showed little interest in the proposed line to the Copperbelt. Northern Rhodesia was now part of the Central African Federation, along with Southern Rhodesia and Nyasaland, and the Southern Rhodesian government was strongly opposed to the construction of a rail link to East Africa which would have diverted traffic away from the route to Beira. The proposed railway between the Copperbelt and Dar es Salaam would, in any case, no longer form part of an imperial throughway. It was left to the new generation of African nationalist leaders to revive discussion of the Tanzam project on the eve of independence.

RAILWAYS AND DEVELOPMENT

Railways transformed communications in Africa during the early years of this century. Until then the human porter had been the main means of transport in East and Central Africa. Human porterage was expensive — costing ten to fifteen times more than rail transport — so only valuable goods, like ivory, could bear the cost. Draught animals were ruled out in much of East Africa because of the tsetse fly, few rivers were navigable over long distances, and the motor car was in its infancy. The railway was therefore often the only economic means of transporting large quantities of goods.

Ambitious plans to build pioneer railways in Africa at the turn of the century were partly sparked off by politico-strategic considerations. At the Berlin Conference in 1885, which met to discuss the Scramble for Africa, the European powers determined that territorial claims would be recognized only if 'effective occupation' was demonstrated. A railway was a particularly permanent feature to back up annexation and colonial administration also required efficient means of transport to provincial centres.

Colonies were not annexed just to paint the map red; they were primarily a means of extracting wealth. One contemporary writer, in a monumental four-volume study of the Cape-to-Cairo project, admitted 'the main function of Africa for many years to come will be the production of raw material for the use of the industrialized world'.[12] Both German East Africa and Northern Rhodesia had originally, after all, been taken over by companies and it was only later that the German and British governments assumed administrative responsibility. Rail outlets became essential to open up Africa's resources, since agricultural produce and minerals had to be transported to coastal ports for shipment to Europe. Areas where cash-crop farming and mining developed then served as new markets for European manufactured goods.

The colonial powers were anxious to develop agricultural production in Africa, both to provide alternative sources for tropical products and to tap a source of tax revenue for covering administrative expenses. Sisal, for example, became increasingly important in German East Africa from the turn of the century and it remained Tanganyika's largest export until the 1960s. The fibre has a low value-to-weight ratio, so it can only be grown economically where rail transport is available. Tanganyika's major agricultural exports are still produced mainly in areas served by the railway network: in some cases lines were specially built to serve regions of high potential (such as the cotton fields around Mwanza) and in other instances (as in the tobacco area near Tabora) production developed because cheap transport was already available. European plantation owners were one of the most vocal groups calling for the construction of new railways, but once a line was built the colonial administration had an interest in encouraging further settlement in order to generate additional traffic and make rail operation more profitable.

Exploitation of mineral resources also required access to rail transport. The Northern Rhodesian mining industry could not have been established until the railway was completed, and without such rich mineral deposits the line would probably not have been built until many years later. Lead and zinc deposits at Broken Hill accounted for the decision to extend the railway from Kalomo. Transit revenue from Katanga's copper encouraged the extension of the line from Broken Hill into the Congo. At this time the size of the Northern Rhodesian copper deposits was not yet realized, so it was fortunate that the main route already passed very close to the Copperbelt. Small branch lines were constructed, mainly between 1929 and 1932, to serve the Northern Rhodesian mines, and copper has since provided the railway with its main source of revenue.

The era of railway construction reached its height between 1900 and 1914. A thousand miles of track were laid in German East Africa and more than 500 miles in Northern Rhodesia. Between the wars a number of important branch lines were constructed in the two countries, totalling almost a thousand miles altogether, but the main pattern of transport routes had already been established. The Tanzam railway has therefore been the first major rail project in Tanzania and Zambia since World War I.

Railway construction in German East Africa and Northern Rhodesia before 1914 largely determined the spatial pattern of development found in the two countries today. The early rail lines set into motion mechanisms that have proved more effective than any subsequent transport routes. Cause and effect are difficult to separate: railways were originally built to areas thought to have good economic prospects, while the absence of cheap communications meant that many regions of reasonable potential remained unexploited. Since World War II road transport has assumed a new importance. Even the road network, however, has been influenced by the railways since denser systems of roads are found along the railways, where they act as feeders, than in those areas not served by rail.

Development is particularly uneven in Northern Rhodesia. The country is divided in half by the line from the Victoria Falls to the Copperbelt and this route is its backbone. Development during the colonial period was overconcentrated in this narrow strip, leaving vast stretches of this huge country (more than three times the size of the United Kingdom) almost untouched. Forty per cent of Northern Rhodesia's people now live within 25 miles of the railway and virtually all the nation's economic activity in the monetary sector, as well as most government services, are located in this narrow strip. A vicious circle developed: people and capital were attracted to the line-of-rail, while the remainder of the country was deprived of the benefits of modernization. Away from the line-of-rail there are few towns (none with a population over 13,000 in 1969), no substantial mines or industry, and the vast majority of the people eke out a meagre living on subsistence agriculture. Similar processes occurred in Tanganyika where development has been concentrated along the two railways built by the Germans before World War I.

The pattern of railway development—from coastal ports to inland centres of economic potential—is a reflection of the fact that the economies of virtually all African states are externally orientated: even today raw materials, both agricultural produce and minerals, are mainly produced for export, rather than to feed local mouths or industries. The colonial powers had little incentive to invest in transport facilities that would have altered the economic structure of their colonies. Dependence, after all, produced large profits. Rail links were therefore built from seaports, so that transport between inland centres, unless they both happened to lie on the same route to the coast, was usually difficult. Existing railway systems therefore sometimes made it cheaper to transport goods to Europe, rather than between distant parts of an African country or to another neighbouring state.

## DAR ES SALAAM TO THE COPPERBELT

Tanganyika Railways, in a rather grandiose gesture, published a timetable for rail and steamer services between Cape Town and Cairo in 1929. The trip, according to the timetable, could be made in only 39 days. Even today it is doubtful if the overland journey could be done much more quickly and, in any case, political problems would make it difficult to cross all eight borders. In 1929 the only section of the route between Dar es Salaam and Cape Town that could not be covered by scheduled rail or steamer services (except with a long detour through the Congo) was between the Lake Tanganyika port of Mpulungu and the Northern Rhodesian railway at Broken Hill. The guidebook remarked that a lorry, taking five days for the journey, occasionally operated on this route.

During the colonial period the only overland link between Tanganyika and Northern Rhodesia was the grandly-titled Great North Road, which had been begun in 1915 to convey British troops and supplies from Northern Rhodesia to the East African front

during World War I. The possibility of building a rail link between
Tanganyika and Northern Rhodesia had been considered on a
number of occasions during the colonial period. But Northern
Rhodesia had been colonized from the south and its foreign trade was
sent across the Victoria Falls Bridge, through Southern Rhodesia, to
ports in Mozambique. This seemed a satisfactory route, at least until
independence, and powerful interests — the colonial administration in
Lusaka, European settlers in Salisbury, Rhodesia Railways, and the
copper companies — had little interest in developing other outlets.
Northern Rhodesia's Northern Province was thought to have very
little economic potential, and besides the region provided a useful
source of labour for the Copperbelt, so there was little reason to build
a railway to Tanganyika.

The south-west of Tanganyika, on the other hand, had much
brighter economic prospects. Extensive mineral deposits were known
to exist in the Southern Highlands. But their exploitation would
have required a railway and the high cost of the line meant that
mining was never begun. Agricultural prospects were also bright,
although again poor transport meant that only a few cash crops could
be grown economically, and some European settlers established
plantations in the Southern Highlands.

The southern half of Tanganyika was seen by the colonial
authorities as a source of labour for plantations in the north. A
colonial head tax was imposed, partly in order to force the Africans to
seek paid employment. Since there were virtually no possibilities of
wage-labour south of the Central Line, this meant that they had to
migrate northwards. In Iringa and Songea districts, for example, it
was estimated in 1925 that around twenty per cent of the male
population was away working in the north. Sir Donald Cameron,
Governor of Tanganyika, was so committed to the policy of keeping
certain parts of the country as labour reserves that once, when
discussing the proposed railway to the south-west, he enquired how it
might facilitate the movement of southern labourers to northern
estates. Migration took away the most productive sector of the
population and actually *under*developed southern Tanganyika.

The much-discussed rail link between Northern Rhodesia and
Tanganyika, originally seen as part of a Cape-to-Cairo line, was
never built during the colonial period because the two territories were
orientated in opposite directions. Northern Rhodesia had been
colonized from the south — this was symbolized by the railway which
was built northwards from Victoria Falls — and much later, in 1953,

the territory became part of the Central African Federation. The two Rhodesias, along with Nyasaland, formed an economic and political unit under the control of European settlers in Salisbury. Northern Rhodesia's economy remained dominated by its southern neighbour, which naturally opposed any moves to reorientate economic ties towards East Africa.

Tanganyika, at least after it fell under British administration, was linked to its northern neighbours of Kenya and Uganda. The three territories formed a common market and later the East Africa High Commission was established to operate shared services, such as the railways. Despite the fact that both Northern Rhodesia and Tanganyika had been British territories since World War I, there was very little contact between them during the colonial era.

The original railway systems in Northern Rhodesia and Tanganyika, as in so many other parts of Africa, set up spatial patterns of development that concentrated the monetary sector almost entirely along the line-of-rail. Frantz Fanon, in his classic study of the impact of imperialism, noted that: 'Colonialism hardly ever exploits the whole of a country. It contents itself with bringing to light the natural resources, which it extracts, and exports to meet the needs of the mother country's industries, thereby allowing certain sectors of the colony to become relatively rich. But the rest of the colony follows its path of underdevelopment and poverty, or at all events sinks into it more deeply.'[13] The new generation of African nationalists who emerged during the 1950s saw the importance of developing their countries to serve national needs, rather than those of their colonial power, and a railway between Dar es Salaam and the Copperbelt appeared an important element in their struggle for freedom.

# II
# ZAMBIA: RHODESIA'S HOSTAGE

'I would like to see in my lifetime a dream of one of the most effective colonialists fulfilled in the service of Africa,' Zambian leader Kenneth Kaunda announced just before his country's independence in 1964.[1] The decision to build a rail link between the Copperbelt and Dar es Salaam had been taken by Kaunda back in 1961, and by independence it had become an important priority of the new Zambian government. But the dream of Rhodes and the hopes of Kaunda were miles apart: the original Northern Rhodesian railway had been 'an instrument of imperialism and colonialism', Kaunda pointed out, while the Tanzam project would be 'a freedom railway, a railway for strengthening African unity and independence'.[2]

'They don't change the names of countries after you die, do they?' Rhodes once asked a friend.[3] Northern Rhodesia, whose name was removed from the map to erase the memory of its founder, won its independence on 24 October 1964. Zambia was named after the Zambezi River, which separates the country from its southern neighbour. The break-up of the Central African Federation, although it brought freedom to Zambia and Malawi, entrenched European settler power in Southern Rhodesia (which became known simply as Rhodesia). Meanwhile the Portuguese government stubbornly maintained that Angola and Mozambique were integral parts of Portugal and would never be granted independence. In South Africa the rising level of African oppression had been brutally demonstrated by the Sharpeville massacre in 1960, which left 67 blacks shot dead after a peaceful protest. Zambia was now in the front line: across the Zambezi River lay white regimes grimly determined to resist demands for majority rule.

On 11 November 1965, just a few days after Zambia had celebrated its first anniversary of independence, Ian Smith illegally proclaimed his country's Unilateral Declaration of Independence. Sanctions were imposed against the rebel regime and guerrilla fighters began the protracted struggle for majority rule. Zambia was in the dangerously vulnerable position of being economically dependent on the very regime it wished to see brought down. Northern Rhodesia had developed as an economic appendage of its southern neighbour and this was symbolized by the fact that virtually all its foreign trade was carried by rail on the southern route. The two Rhodesias were like Siamese twins, joined together by the Victoria Falls Bridge, with the white settlers of Salisbury in control. Freedom from Britain and disengagement from the white South were seen by the new Zambian government as two sides of the same political coin.

Zambia's traditional rail outlet to the sea, across Rhodesia and Mozambique, now ran through enemy territory. Zambia, after suffering a series of disruptions in using the line and having decided to disengage from the white South, began to develop alternative routes for its foreign trade. These mainly proved to be expensive, lacked sufficient capacity, and were politically unreliable. It became increasingly clear that only a rail outlet to Tanzania (as Tanganyika was called after the union with Zanzibar in 1964) would preserve Zambia's independence. There were, in addition, strong economic justifications for building the rail link to Dar es Salaam in order to open up vast areas of the two countries which had been neglected during the colonial era.

## THE DREAM REVIVED

Kaunda addressed a mass rally on the Copperbelt and told the excited crowd in April 1961 of the dynamic programme of economic development that would follow independence. Most important of all would be the construction of a rail link to Tanganyika. During the independence struggle warm ties had quickly been formed between the major nationalist parties in the two countries—the Tanganyika African National Union (TANU) and the United National Independence Party of Northern Rhodesia (UNIP)—and their leaders, Julius Nyerere and Kenneth Kaunda, met frequently for informal discussions. Tanganyika became the first of the British territories in the region to achieve independence, winning its freedom on 9 December 1961, so TANU was able to play a particularly important role in assisting nationalist parties in neighbouring countries.

Back in 1954 Kaunda had attempted to arrange a meeting of African nationalists from East and Central Africa and, although the conference was never held, four years later the Pan-African Freedom Movement of East and Central Africa was set up. TANU and UNIP were both key members of this organization, established to co-ordinate the independence struggles taking place within the region, and this provided an additional forum for bringing the two parties closer together. TANU, after it became the ruling party in independent Tanganyika, was able to give financial assistance to UNIP, particularly during the 1962 and 1964 election campaigns in Northern Rhodesia, and although the sums provided were relatively small they represented a symbolic demonstration of solidarity. Nyerere also took every opportunity, especially during his visits to London, to put pressure on Britain to break up the Central African Federation and grant independence to African governments in each of the three territories.

Nyerere was the only President to attend Zambia's independence celebrations and by then TANU and UNIP had already become close allies. The new generation of African leaders were concerned that the relationships inherited from the colonial period should not determine the pattern of relations after independence. Northern Rhodesia's economic ties had been orientated southwards, while Tanganyika had faced northwards to East Africa. But African unity demanded that functional links should be developed between neighbouring black states.

Economic ties between Zambia and Tanzania were almost non-existent. In 1964 trade amounted to only £100,000 in each direction. This was partly due to the absence of cheap transport links—cargo was normally sent from Dar es Salaam on a 2,500-mile journey by sea to Mozambique and then by rail through Rhodesia—so a direct rail link appeared essential to the new governments in Lusaka and Dar es Salaam. More cautious economists pointed out that a railway would not automatically lead to economic integration. But without an improvement in transport facilities it was difficult to see how economic co-operation could be strengthened.

Kaunda and Nyerere were also determined to develop areas of their countries which had lain neglected during the colonial period. Economic growth in Northern Rhodesia had been concentrated along the railway that ran northwards from Victoria Falls to the Copperbelt. If the original railway through Northern Rhodesia had led to substantial development, would not a new link to Dar es Salaam have a similar impact on the eastern half of the country? Superficially this was an attractive argument, but the fact was that circumstances had changed. The old line had been built before the motor-car era, so most towns had grown up along the railway, and the area between the Falls and the Copperbelt included regions of good agricultural potential. Lusaka had prospered, particularly towards the end of the colonial period, because of its role as capital. Copper deposits, which form the basis of the Zambian economy, happened to be found close to the existing railway and this is the major reason why development is now so heavily concentrated along the original line-of-rail.

The Northern Province, which would be served by the proposed rail link to Tanzania, was a neglected area and the lack of transport facilities had undoubtedly been a serious constraint to development. Kasama, the provincial capital, was almost 600 miles from Lusaka, almost all over dirt roads, and its remoteness from the economic and political centres of the country merely perpetuated its underdevelopment. But the Northern Province lacked most of the factors which had led to development along the original railway between Victoria Falls and the Copperbelt. Soils are generally infertile, so that the land only sustains a sparse population living on a primitive system of shifting agriculture, and no commercially exploitable mineral deposits have been found along the Tanzam route. A railway through the Northern Province would not, by itself, lead to dramatic developments—but improved transport should provide an essential precondition for growth.

The rail link to Dar es Salaam was an important priority of UNIP's programme—it was featured in the party's election manifestos in 1962 and 1964—but the project was criticized by the opposition Northern Rhodesian African National Congress (ANC). The ANC's main base of support, the Southern Province, had benefited from its position astride the rail route to Salisbury and the party, which was less hostile towards Southern Rhodesia, argued that existing lines were sufficient for the country's needs. Although relations with Tanganyika were close, this could not be regarded as a permanent feature and, since construction of the Tanzam project would be very expensive, the capital would be better employed on improving internal communications within Northern Rhodesia.

The indecisive result of the October 1962 election forced UNIP and the ANC to form a coalition government in order to prevent Sir Roy Welensky's Federal Party from retaining power. The Transport Ministry was allocated to an ANC member, F. N. Stubbs, who kept this post until the January 1964 elections gave UNIP total control. Stubbs described the Tanzam railway as a white elephant and little serious consideration was given to the project by the Northern Rhodesian government until the year of independence.

'If Dr Kaunda calls you to carry copper on your shoulders to Dar es Salaam', one Zambian politician exhorted his followers, just before independence, 'if he wakes you up at night to prepare roads . . . be ready to do so instantaneously.'⁴ Freedom certainly generated great enthusiasm to develop the country and sparked off a revolution of rising expectations. Many Africans naively believed that changing the colour of the occupant of State House would make their country, and themselves, visibly wealthier overnight. Kaunda realized the need to channel the energy and expectations of his people: the Tanzam railway was a bold project to provide large-scale employment and open up areas which had been neglected during the colonial period.

In Tanganyika too, economic development had been concentrated along the main railway routes in the north and centre. The new Tanganyikan government, whose leader pledged on the eve of independence to do more to develop the nation in ten years than the colonialists had done in forty, was particularly anxious to open up the southern half of the country. The Tanzam railway represented a massive project to match the hopes of independence.

The proposed rail route would pass through areas with excellent agricultural potential. The Kilombero Valley, known as 'the ricebowl of Tanganyika', was an especially fertile region and a UN Food and Agriculture Organization (FAO) report in 1961 proposed that 820,000 acres could be brought under cultivation by the end of the century. The line would then climb up the wooded Mufindi escarpment, where preliminary investigations had suggested that a massive pulp and paper mill could be established. The Southern Highlands, a region in many respects similar to the rich Kenyan Highlands, had fertile volcanic soils and adequate rainfall which supported a comparatively dense population. Cash crops— particularly tea, coffee, and pyrethrum—were grown over much of the Highlands and these brought in valuable foreign exchange. The FAO report also proposed that in just one area in southern Tanganyika, the Usangu Plains, up to 520,000 acres could be cultivated. Substantial mineral wealth—particularly coal, iron ore, and limestone—was known to exist in south-west Tanganyika. There had been no industrial development in the southern half of the country, so these deposits offered a unique opportunity to develop a neglected part of Tanganyika, as well as to establish a heavy industrial sector.

No large-scale agricultural or industrial development could take place without an improvement in transport facilities. Asphalting the

Great North Road could have a catalytic effect in opening up the area. But some projects—such as large-scale irrigation schemes in the Kilombero and Usangu Valleys, the paper plant, and mineral exploitation—would require a railway to become economic. A line to Northern Rhodesia would also open up a rich market on the Copperbelt for southern Tanganyika's agricultural and industrial output.

At independence the governments of Tanganyika and Zambia both inherited economies which had been developed to serve European needs. There were islands of development, it is true, but in a sea of underdevelopment. This was reflected in the pattern of transport routes, particularly railways, which had been established during the colonial era. The construction of a rail link from the Copperbelt to Dar es Salaam, passing for nearly 1,200 miles through areas with poor communications, should have a great impact on the development of these remote areas. The argument for the new railway was often oversimplified—if railways had opened up Africa at the turn of the century then, it was said, the Tanzam line should have a similar effect—but the project did appear to be an important move towards reorientating the economies of the two African states towards a more meaningful independence.

## HOSTAGE OF THE SOUTH

By the early 1960s the two Rhodesias were treading diverging paths towards independence. In Southern Rhodesia the European settler community, representing only one twentieth of the population, was gaining further power at the expense of the African majority, and Winston Field, leader of the Rhodesian Front, became Prime Minister in December 1962 on a platform supporting settler interests. By the following year Field's party had become increasingly impatient with his attempt to win independence through legal means and in April 1964 he was replaced by Ian Smith. Southern Rhodesia was moving quickly on the path towards UDI.

In Northern Rhodesia UNIP swept to power in the January 1964 elections and independence was won on 24 October 1964. Political freedom was attained but the country remained economically dependent on its southern neighbour. Thirty-eight per cent of Zambian imports came from Southern Rhodesia, with an additional twenty-two per cent from South Africa. Copper mining, providing almost half of Zambia's national income, relied on energy from Rhodesia—coal from Wankie (40 miles south of the Victoria Falls),

Kariba electricity (from the south bank of the Zambezi), and oil from
the Umtali refinery (near the Mozambican border). The refined
copper was all exported via Rhodesia to Beira and Lourenço
Marques. Rhodesia Railways (RR) was Zambia's lifeline to the outside
world, with ninety-seven per cent of the nation's foreign trade passing
over the narrow steel girders of the Victoria Falls Bridge.

RR, which owned and operated the rail system in the two
Rhodesias, was one of the few inter-territorial organizations (along
with Central African Airways and the Power Corporation) to survive
the dissolution of the Central African Federation. Control of RR
theoretically lay with the Higher Authority, consisting of two
ministers from each territory, but because of political tensions this
body never effectively met. In practice RR was run by European
administrative staff at its Bulawayo headquarters. Racial problems
were a constant source of disruptions. In March 1964 Northern
Rhodesian railway workers went on strike in protest against RR's
refusal to transfer a white employee who had been involved in a
dispute with an African worker. Then in August it was the turn of the
Europeans to strike over the compulsory posting of a group of white
railwaymen to Northern Rhodesia.

By mid-1965 Southern Rhodesia was on the brink of UDI and
tensions over RR were coming to a head. In August Ian Smith
claimed that Rhodesia was subsidizing Zambian traffic to the tune of
£1 million a year. This charge was refuted by a detailed study,
published a few months later by the Brookings Institute in
Washington, which showed that Zambian cargo accounted for only
eight per cent of RR's tonnage, but brought in twenty-eight per cent
of the revenue.[5]

The Rhodesian Transport Minister, George Rutland, accused
Zambia of hoarding freight wagons, a remark which clearly revealed
the Rhodesian wish to split up the jointly-owned system. Rutland had
in fact sent a confidential message to his Zambian counterpart four
months earlier proposing the division of RR at Victoria Falls. This
initiative led to the first meeting of the railway's Higher Authority on
8 November 1965 at the Falls Hotel. Zambia was only agreeable to
dividing the system if the assets were split on an equal basis — which
was unacceptable to Rhodesia — so a settlement seemed remote.
Three days after discussions began Zambian officials woke up to find
that their Rhodesian counterparts had disappeared: they had
hurriedly left for Salisbury to hear Smith's proclamation of
independence.

'UDI was a time bomb,' commented the former American ambassador to Zambia. 'The mechanism was triggered in Salisbury; but the explosive was in Lusaka and on the Copperbelt.'[6] The bang came on 11 November 1965 with Smith's declaration that a blow had been struck 'for the preservation of justice, civilization and Christianity'.[7] Many whites working on the Zambian Copperbelt, two thirds of whom originated from Southern Rhodesia or South Africa, gleefully celebrated the event. European locomotive drivers on the Copperbelt greeted the UDI announcement with prolonged blasts on their whistles, an ominous warning of the dangerous times ahead, and only two weeks later white railwaymen, mostly from Rhodesia, went on strike at Livingstone after a racial incident involving Zambian youths.

Rhodesia was technically a British colony, although in practice it had had internal self-government since 1923, so crushing the rebel regime was clearly a British responsibility. Kaunda believed that Britain should use force, if necessary, to re-establish its authority and, despite the risks involved, the Zambian leader offered his territory as a base to launch a military operation against Rhodesia. The British government, however, had already declared that the use of force would not be considered. Wilson's critics believed that his most powerful card had been thrown away. As many Africans remarked, Britain had not shrunk from using force in many other colonial territories.

Wilson had only one card left to play: sanctions. In January 1966 the British Prime Minister told his Commonwealth colleagues that economic sanctions would bring Smith to his knees 'within a matter of weeks rather than months'.[8] The weeks dragged on into months, the months into years, and in 1975 Smith celebrated the first decade of independence. A series of measures were introduced to break off many of Britain's economic links with the rebel regime. There was, however, a disturbing lack of planning and political judgement in Whitehall and Downing Street. It was not until December 1966, more than a year after UDI, that Britain went to the UN to request mandatory sanctions, and these only covered certain products until they were made comprehensive in May 1968. British policy was 'sanctions on instalment' and by the time these had all been introduced the Smith regime had found that South Africa and Portugal, working with businessmen all round the world, were happy to turn a blind eye to sanctions-busting.

Paradoxically it was Rhodesian UDI, upholding Rhodes' principle of white supremacy, that in the end broke off contact across the Victoria Falls Bridge. Soon afterwards British and Zambian officials discussed plans for a 'quick kill' involving an overnight ban on Zambian imports from Rhodesia. The Rhodesian regime would presumably reply by cutting off Zambia's foreign trade, so emergency measures would have to be taken to keep the Zambian economy afloat. The plan was shelved after the British government refused to undertake to bear all the additional expenses that these measures would have entailed. Talk of a 'quick kill' was briefly revived a few months later during a British minister's visit to Lusaka. By this time Kaunda had become very disillusioned with Britain's attitude towards Rhodesia, which he regarded as totally irresponsible, and the plan was quickly buried. 'To hear you speaking in terms of limited cash commitments and expenditure ceilings', a Zambian permanent secretary told a visiting British minister, 'is like quibbling over the cost of a blood transfusion . . . our risks are open-ended'.[9]

Because Zambia was committed to majority rule Kaunda felt obliged, as far as was feasible, to support sanctions against the rebel regime. But Zambia was in the front line. It was a standing joke among white expatriates on the Copperbelt that sanctions were working very well indeed . . . in Zambia. Reducing trade with Rhodesia, along with disruptions to Zambia's traditional rail outlet to the sea, has cost the Zambian government an enormous sum which has been only partly recouped from foreign donors.

Virtually all of Zambia's foreign trade passed over the Victoria Falls Bridge. There was therefore the constant danger that Rhodesia would retaliate by closing this route, and in August 1964, more than a year before UDI, Kaunda announced that a plot had been uncovered to blockade Zambia by cutting the rail link. UDI only strengthened Kaunda's belief that it was essential to build a new route to the sea. A railway through Tanzania to Dar es Salaam was necessary to provide the new nation with a secure outlet for its foreign trade.

Every day seventeen oil wagons rumbled across the Falls Bridge, carrying Zambia's entire petroleum requirements from the Rhodesian refinery at Umtali. Just a month after UDI the British government imposed an oil embargo against Rhodesia and the Salisbury regime immediately cut off Zambia's supply. Emergency measures—first an airlift and then road haulage from Dar es Salaam—had to be taken to keep Zambia supplied until a pipeline was built. At one point, early in January 1966, there was only three days' supply of petroleum left in the country. The oil embargo against Rhodesia demonstrated Zambia's vulnerability, as well as Rhodesia's ability to survive: while petroleum was airlifted at enormous expense to keep Zambia alive, the Rhodesian regime was obtaining sufficient supplies through Mozambique and South Africa. Within a few months of UDI it was the Zambian economy that was in danger of collapse. Rhodesia, with the active support of Portugal and South Africa, seemed able to readjust to the new situation.

In April 1966 the Zambian government suddenly announced that it would no longer permit the transfer of funds from the RR office in Zambia to its Bulawayo headquarters. Much of this money, amounting to £1 million a month, originated from Zambian copper exports and the government claimed that this move was intended to deny the rebel regime an important source of funds. It was clear, however, that Zambia's unilateral decision would result in Rhodesian retaliation — presumably the closure of the railway to Zambian traffic.

Kaunda's decision, only a few weeks after the Labour Party had been returned to power with an increased majority in London, was interpreted as an attempt to precipitate Britain into taking decisive action against Smith. Almost half of Britain's copper imports came from Zambia, the only major exporter in the Sterling Area, so shortages could have led to massive unemployment in Britain and much higher copper prices. Disruption of copper exports might therefore have pressurized Britain into taking more active measures against Smith.

At the end of May the Rhodesian authorities reacted to Zambia's refusal to transfer RR funds by demanding advance payment for transit charges. Zambia initially refused, but without coal supplies from Wankie, then running at nearly a million tons a year, it would have been forced to curtail copper production. Within a few days Kaunda had agreed to pay coal transport costs in advance. Zambia's exports were now cut off, while imports from Rhodesia continued, which was exactly the reverse of what sanctions were intended to achieve. Some copper was sent out by alternative routes, such as the Great North Road to Dar es Salaam and the Benguela railway to Lobito, but these could only carry about a third of the Copperbelt's production. The Rhodesians knew their strength, and, by the time £20 million worth of copper had been stockpiled, the Zambian government was forced to concede. A face-saving device was then arranged whereby copper consumers paid Rhodesian transit costs via a Swiss bank. On 25 July 1966, two months after copper shipments through Rhodesia had been halted, the freight wagons with the valuable copper wirebars once more began to cross the Falls Bridge.

During the early months of 1966, when it appeared likely that the joint railway system would be divided, the Rhodesians and the Zambians both tried to retain as much rolling stock as possible. A one-for-one swap was quickly instituted whereby equal numbers of wagons were exchanged at Victoria Falls. Both countries suffered from a shortage of rolling stock; Rhodesia found it difficult to purchase new equipment because of sanctions, and Zambia had problems in sending rolling stock for repair to the Bulawayo workshop. The shortage of locomotives and rolling stock hit Zambia's foreign trade. Coal supplies from Wankie (essential for copper refining) were disrupted, so that copper production had to be cut back by almost a third during late 1966 and early 1967; at the beginning of 1967 RR placed a temporary embargo on the acceptance of Zambia's imports from Mozambique on the grounds that there were insufficient Zambian locomotives to haul the freight over the Victoria Falls; and a shortage of freight wagons limited cargo sent on the Benguela line to Lobito.

Growing tensions between Zambia and Rhodesia made dissolution of the jointly-owned RR system almost inevitable. Under the agreement which had been signed by the two Rhodesias in December 1963 it was specifically stated that 'the ownership of the Railways . . . will be with the two Governments in equal shares'.[10] But Rhodesia demanded a larger share of the railway's assets — worth over £100 million — so formal negotiations on the break-up of the rail system, which began in November 1966, ended in stalemate. In mid-1967 there was a de facto division of RR into two systems.

Zambia Railways (ZR) was established on 1 July 1967, with its headquarters at Kabwe (formerly known as Broken Hill), to operate the 500 miles of track from Victoria Falls northwards to the Copperbelt. Zambia only inherited a small proportion of RR's rolling stock — 87 of the 403 locomotives and 1,200 of the 13,000 freight wagons — so purchases had to be made abroad. Since the main RR workshop was located in Rhodesia at Bulawayo, a new £6-million repair workshop was established at Kabwe. ZR also lost most of its skilled European employees — only 157 out of more than 1,000 remained — which caused short-term difficulties. From 1968 to 1970 a team from Sudan Railways was brought in to manage ZR, but they were unable to deal with the problems created by the break-up of RR, and in 1971 they were replaced by a group from the Canadian

National Railways. Under the Canadian team the efficiency of the rail system in Zambia has been gradually improved.

Once RR was divided, the Rhodesian authorities were able to increase charges for handling Zambian traffic. Costs for general imports were raised by about 20 per cent, copper export tariffs went up by a third, and in March 1968 the rate for Wankie coal was more than tripled. In October 1968 Rhodesia announced that charges for general goods would be increased but, after negotiations with Zambia, it was announced that this would only be enforced if copper exports fell below 25,000 tons a month. This surcharge was applied for only a short time, between March and May 1971, but Zambia thereby remained tied to exporting almost half its copper production through Rhodesia. Until Zambia had alternative routes to the sea she was in a weak position to resist Rhodesia's demands for higher rates.

Zambia was doubly landlocked. Dependence on transport routes through Rhodesia also involved reliance on railways and harbours in Portuguese-controlled Mozambique. This was particularly dangerous since Zambia supported two liberation movements—FRELIMO (Front for the Liberation of Mozambique) and the much smaller COREMO (Revolutionary Committee for Mozambique)—which were fighting to overthrow Portuguese colonial rule. As early as December 1965 the Portuguese government had threatened to close Beira (as well as the Angolan port of Lobito) to Zambian traffic if Lusaka did not hand over FRELIMO fighters who had allegedly killed two Portuguese during a raid in Mozambique. Zambia replied that there was no evidence that the FRELIMO fighters had operated from its territory and Portugal never actually implemented its threat.

A more serious situation arose in March 1971 when Portugal claimed that five civilians, captured by COREMO during a raid on Mozambique, had been taken to Zambia. The Zambian government denied that the Portuguese were being held on its territory. But Beira dockworkers, with the tacit consent of the authorities, declared a partial boycott of Zambian goods. Zambia was then importing large quantities of grain, because of the failure of its maize harvest, and was therefore in a particularly vulnerable position until the embargo was lifted a few weeks later. The crisis was a reminder of the pressures that Portugal—through its control of railways and harbours in Mozambique and Angola—was able to exert on landlocked Zambia.

### ESCAPE FROM DEPENDENCE

Since independence Zambia has suffered from constant disruptions in its use of the rail route through Rhodesia and Mozambique. Zambia could have adopted a more conciliatory attitude towards the white regimes of Southern Africa, particularly Rhodesia, in a way similar to that of Malawi. A 'business as usual' approach would no doubt have avoided many of the difficulties following UDI. Kaunda, however, is a man of strong principles and has taken a firm stand against minority rule in Southern Africa. It is also in Zambia's long-term interests to reduce its economic dependence on Rhodesia in order to establish a more self-reliant economy.

Economic dependence could easily compromise political independence. Zambia's militant approach to the liberation struggle in Southern Africa might well be limited by its reliance on economic ties with the minority regimes. Disengagement from the white South was therefore a vital priority of the Zambian government. Both the establishment of import-substitution industries and diversification of economic relations, particularly with black African states to the north, were essential elements in this strategy.

The amount of Zambia's imports that came from Rhodesia fell from forty per cent in 1965 to only two per cent eight years later (from £31 million to £4 million). Zambia's major imports from Rhodesia at UDI were two vital sources of energy, coal and electricity. The copper industry was originally dependent on Wankie coal. But since 1966 domestic sources of coal have been opened up, so that by 1971 Zambia had become virtually self-sufficient. The Zambian government has also invested in several hydro-electric projects which reduced the country's dependence on the Kariba plant. Apart from declining amounts of electricity, Zambian imports from Rhodesia have been negligible since 1973.

Many of Zambia's traditional imports from Rhodesia were initially replaced by South African products. Imports from South Africa rose slightly from £21 million in 1965 to £25 eight years later. As a percentage of Zambia's total imports, however, this represented a substantial decline from 20% to 12%. Zambia has never had extensive trade with Mozambique and Angola. The Zambian government has therefore been remarkably successful in reducing its economic dependence on imports from the white regimes of Southern Africa.

Another major factor in reducing economic dependence on Rhodesia has been the development of alternative routes for Zambia's foreign trade. The Copperbelt is located in the heart of Central Africa, approximately equidistant from the Indian and Atlantic Oceans, and as the crow flies the two coasts are both around 700 miles away. The actual distance by rail to Beira, the traditional route, is twice as far. Short-term emergencies—such as the oil blockade and the 1966 payments crisis—as well as the longer-term need to reduce dependence on Rhodesia, meant that the Zambian government had to explore the development of new routes.

The nature of Zambia's foreign trade caused a number of problems in developing new transport routes. First, an unusually low proportion of Zambia's external commerce—3 per cent in 1972—is with neighbouring countries, so access to the sea is vital. Secondly, Zambia's level of trade is relatively high compared with many African states—it is more than twice as large as Tanzania's (for a population only a third of the size). Finally, there is an imbalance between exports and imports: in 1972 exports (almost entirely copper) amounted to 791,000 tons and imports, at 1,953,000 tons (including 504,000 tons of oil), were more than twice the weight. Despite these difficulties, disengagement from the white South and diversification away from a single route became the twin policies of the Zambian government.

## NEW ROUTES TO THE WEST

Zambia already had a second rail route to the sea which ran from the Copperbelt, through the Congo and Angola, to the excellent harbour at Lobito. In 1936 the Northern Rhodesian copper companies had signed a twenty-year agreement with RR under which they undertook to send out all their production through Southern Rhodesia in exchange for lower rates for copper exports and imports of Wankie coal. This meant that during the colonial period Northern Rhodesia made very little use of the Benguela line to Lobito. In 1956, when the original agreement expired, new arrangements were made between the three railway companies operating in the Rhodesias, the Congo, and Angola. A small proportion of Northern Rhodesian copper (up to a maximum of 20 per cent) could be exported via the shorter Benguela route with freight rates, whether to ports in Mozambique or Angola, fixed at the same level. By 1960 RR, worried by the loss of this traffic to the Benguela railway, unilaterally offered a discount rate of £9.53 a ton (compared with the agreed rate of £14.85) for copper then being routed via Lobito. The copper companies naturally took advantage of this agreement, so at independence Zambia was sending little traffic on the Benguela line.

After UDI, and in particular during the payments crisis with RR in 1966, Zambia once again began to use the Benguela route. By

1966/7 about 10 per cent of its general imports and 25 per cent of its copper exports were being shipped via Angola. There were, however, serious limitations to the capacity of this route. Steam locomotives, burning eucalyptus wood, were still used (although the change-over to diesels began in 1967) and there was a shortage of freight wagons to handle Zambia's sudden requirements.

The most serious bottleneck was a stretch of track near the Atlantic coast where the railway climbs up the escarpment and only a small number of freight wagons could be hauled up the steep route at a time. Because of increasing traffic on the Benguela line, and in particular because of greater Zambian use of this route, the decision was taken during 1968 to improve the track between the coast and the town of Cubal. The Cubal Variant, as it is called, reduced the distance of this section from 115 to 80 miles and the £16-million improvement, completed in October 1974, has greatly increased the capacity of the Benguela line.

Along with the decision to proceed with the Cubal Variant, a proposal was discussed to build a £19-million rail link between the Zambian Copperbelt and the Lobito line in Angola which would by-pass the Congo. In addition to being slightly shorter, this route, which had been considered since the 1920s, would have had two main advantages for Zambia. First, it would have provided the North-western Province of Zambia, an area which even today has no tarred roads, with better transport facilities. It was also expected that the railway would make it more economic to exploit copper deposits along the route at Kansanshi and Lumwana. There was speculation that Tanganyika Concessions, the company which owns Benguela Railways, was particularly concerned that the Zambia-Angola link should be built because it held a seven per cent interest in the Kansanshi mine.

The second reason for Zambian interest in the direct rail link in Angola was that it would have by-passed the Congo and reduced Zambian dependence on a country that had been, at least during the early 1960s, facing acute internal political tensions. Katanga, the province adjoining the Zambian Copperbelt, had seceded from the Congo when independence was granted by Belgium in 1960 and it was not until January 1963 that secession was ended. Moise Tshombe, the reactionary Katangan leader supported by Union Minière (which owned the Katangan copper mines), had also maintained close links with the Zambian opposition party, the African National Congress. In July 1964 Tshombe regained power, this time as

Congolese Prime Minister in Kinshasa, and until his fall in October 1965 Zambian-Congolese relations remained strained. Further tensions within the Congo continued to disrupt communications. On 12 June 1967 a group of Belgian mercenaries based in Angola sabotaged the Lubidi bridge on the railway through Katanga, interrupting traffic for six weeks until repairs were made. Political chaos in the Congo meant that transport routes through that strife-torn country were unreliable.

Early in 1969 the head of Benguela Railways, one of the few Portuguese to be received in Lusaka, was granted a personal interview with Kaunda to discuss the proposed Angola-Zambia rail link. China had already promised to build the Tanzam railway but, since the Chinese survey had not yet been completed, Benguela Railways were presumably making a final attempt to secure Zambia's valuable transit trade. If the Zambian government had accepted the offer of a direct link to Angola it would, no doubt, have had to undertake not to go ahead with the Tanzam project or at least to make sure that a large proportion of Zambian traffic was allocated to the Lobito route. This would have resulted in greater dependence on Angola, still under colonial rule, and have provided the Portuguese government with a powerful means of pressure to discourage Zambia from supporting the Angolan liberation movements.

In the early 1960s guerrilla warfare was begun in Angola against Portuguese colonial rule. Two of the liberation movements, MPLA (Popular Movement for the Liberation of Angola) and UNITA (National Union for the Total Independence of Angola), later occupied parts of the country along the route of the Benguela railway. Since this was Angola's most important transport link, which was also extensively used for transporting Portuguese troops, the line became an obvious target for sabotage.

Attacks on the Benguela railway unfortunately also had a serious impact on Angola's two independent neighbours, Zambia and the Congo, which provided most of the line's freight (86 per cent in 1972). Whenever the track was destroyed traffic had to be held up until repairs had been made and, even when the line was operating, the route's capacity was reduced in eastern Angola because trains only operated during daylight hours to reduce the danger of attack. The Benguela line was first seriously damaged on Christmas Eve in 1966. After a particularly serious attack in March 1967 the Portuguese government retaliated by closing the Angolan-Congolese border for three weeks 'both as a protest and warning to the countries from whose border the saboteurs were believed to have infiltrated'.[11] Since the Benguela route carried a significant proportion of Zambia's trade, Kaunda was forced to bow to Portuguese pressure. The Zambian government withdrew the residence permit of UNITA's president, whose party had organized most of the attacks, and the liberation movement's Lusaka office was closed.

Sabotage of the railway continued regularly until 1970. According to Portuguese government sources in just one four-month period, between January and April 1969, no less than 110 attacks disrupted traffic. During the following month the railway was closed for 25 days when a culvert was destroyed. The magnitude of fighting along the line is suggested by Benguela Railways' announcement that up until 1971 46 of its employees had been killed in clashes with guerrillas. The route has been attacked much less frequently since then. UNITA was attempting to win recognition from the Zambian government, so presumably the liberation movement was reluctant to hit one of Zambia's major transport routes.

The Portuguese authorities also had other methods of putting pressure on Zambia. In March 1970 two trains carrying Zambian goods were systematically looted in Angola. Although it was claimed that these incidents were the spontaneous reactions of outraged citizens following a guerrilla attack on a border post, there may well have been an element of official encouragement. While Angola continued to be ruled by the Portuguese colonial administration — and the Zambian government supported the liberation movements — it was dangerous to remain dependent on the railway to Lobito. In the short run, however, diversion away from RR led to greater dependence on the rail route through Angola — in rather the same way that reducing imports from Rhodesia temporarily resulted in greater trade with South Africa — but this was seen as a necessary stage until the completion of the Tanzam line to Dar es Salaam.

One route that avoided dependence on the Portuguese territories was the rail-river outlet through the Congo to the port of Matadi. Henry Stanley, after he crossed Central Africa from Zanzibar to the River Congo mouth in 999 days a century ago, is supposed to have commented that 'the Congo without a railway isn't worth a penny'. This advice has been followed by Congolese rulers from King Leopold II to Mobuto Seso Seko, who have put great efforts into improvement of the Voie Nationale (National Route) from the Katangan copper mines to the Atlantic. The 1,900-mile route begins at the Zambian border where the railway hauls traffic to the river port of Ilebo. Barges then carry freight down the Kasai and Congo Rivers to Kinshasa, where cargo is railed to the port of Matadi at the mouth of the River Congo.

During the dry season the water level sometimes becomes too low, making it impossible for barges to travel between Ilebo and Kinshasa, while the port of Matadi suffers from silting and is often badly congested. The Voie Nationale is not only slow and relatively expensive, because of the need to trans-ship, but it also lacks the capacity to handle all the Katanga's traffic. It is mainly because of Congolese government policy, stressing the importance of a national route for strategic reasons, that the Voie Nationale is used at all for long-distance traffic. Zambia has therefore utilized the route for only a negligible proportion of her foreign trade.

Since the 1960s serious consideration has been given to improving the Voie Nationale by building a rail link between Ilebo and Kinshasa, eliminating the river section of the route. In 1975 it was announced that an Anglo-Belgian consortium was to build a rail link between Ilebo and Kinshasa. Lonrho, one of the members of the consortium, had previously been interested in constructing the Tanzam line. In addition a group of Japanese firms is to extend the railway from Matadi to the excellent harbour at Port Banana. When these projects are completed, probably in the early 1980s, they will link the Zambian Copperbelt to another Atlantic port. An improved Voie Nationale would offer Zambia an alternative outlet to the sea, provided that sufficient capacity was available after Zaire's traffic had been carried, but charges would almost certainly be higher than on the Tanzam link because of the considerably greater distance involved.

## ZAMBIA TURNS EAST

Tanzania was the most politically reliable outlet for Zambia's foreign trade. Great efforts have therefore been made to improve communications between the two countries, both in order to deal with the immediate needs after UDI and to develop cheap transport facilities for the long term. Immediately after UDI, Dar es Salaam, in addition to Nairobi and Kinshasa, became a major base for flying in Zambia's oil requirements. The British airlift continued until October 1966. But it proved very expensive—with more oil being consumed by the planes (fuelled in Dar es Salaam) than was actually brought into Ndola—so road transport was used as soon as sufficient petroleum stocks had been built up in Zambia.

Zambia Air Cargoes, a subsidiary of Roan Selection Trust (one of the two major copper companies), was established in February 1966 to airlift copper out to Dar es Salaam and carry oil on the return journey. The company operated five Lockheed Hercules aircraft, three purchased by Roan Selection Trust and two by the Zambian government, which were brought from the United States for £1 million each. Air transport costs were very high and, after losses of more than £1 million had piled up three years later, Zambia Air Cargoes was disbanded. Zambia's transport problems threw up all sorts of bizarre suggestions, with the London *Guardian* proposing that a fleet of airships should float Zambia's copper to Tanzanian ports.

The long-term solution to Zambia's fuel needs was a pipeline to Dar es Salaam. Kaunda approached the British government soon after UDI. But Wilson replied that the pipeline would be too expensive (probably costing almost £40 million) and it would take 'a very long time' to complete (mentioning that the 200-miles Beira-Umtali pipeline had taken two years to build).[12] Zambia then turned to Italy and the 1,058 mile pipeline, the longest in Africa, was built at breakneck speed and finished in seventeen months at a cost of only £16 million. The capital was raised by a consortium of Italian banks, headed by Mediobanca, and the line was built by the state oil company ENI (Ente Nationale Indrocarburi). The pipeline is owned by Tanzama Pipelines Limited, two thirds of the shares being held by Zambia and one third by the Tanzanian government.

Zambia's oil crisis once more brought the British company of Lonrho — which has been interested in a number of major transport projects in Central Africa since the 1960s — back into the news. The Lonrho-owned Beira-Umtali pipeline, originally used to import Zambia's requirements into Rhodesia, had just been completed early in 1965. The British government ordered Lonrho to close the £4-million pipeline after an oil embargo was imposed against Rhodesia. Zambia then had to bring in supplies by road from Dar es Salaam and some of this was hauled by Smith and Youngson, a road transport company owned by Lonrho until its nationalization by the Zambian government in 1969. The country's long-term needs could only be met with a pipeline from Dar es Salaam, and Lonrho apparently fought hard to win the contract for this project until it was, in the end, awarded to the Italians.

With the completion of the pipeline in August 1968 the problem of supplying Zambia's oil requirements was resolved. The

Great North Road could then carry larger amounts of other imports for Zambia. The opening of the pipeline also meant that Zambia's largest import — amounting to over 800,000 tons by 1974 — would not need to be carried on the proposed Tanzam railway. In any case Zambia's petroleum consumption was already by the mid-1960s reaching levels where it would have become economic to send oil by pipeline.

'Hell Run' was how the truck drivers described the Great North Road. At UDI almost all the road was still unpaved and it sometimes became impassable during the rainy season. After the oil embargo against Rhodesia, lorries rumbled down the Great North Road carrying supplies until the opening of the pipeline and, following the payments crisis with RR, increasing amounts of copper were also transported by road to Dar es Salaam. The dirt highway quickly deteriorated under the constant pounding of the heavy lorries and the verge soon became littered with broken-down wrecks. During the first half of 1968 the road became virtually impassable.

The Great North Road needed urgent improvements, and back in May 1964, even before UDI had made it a vital lifeline for Zambia, the World Bank had suggested that the route should be upgraded. At this time just over half the stretch between Dar es Salaam and Iringa was paved and the World Bank had agreed to finance the remaining 110 miles. The other 850 miles between Iringa and the Zambian line-of-rail were gravel, so the World Bank recommended that the two sections carrying most traffic — from Iringa to Mbeya and from Kapiri Mposhi to Mpika — should be asphalted and the intermediate gravel stretch improved. The cost of upgrading the sections of the Great North Road most heavily used was estimated at £8 million, but if it was subsequently decided to tar the intermediate section this would call for an additional £4 million.

The World Bank study was produced before the UDI emergency made it essential for the road to be asphalted for its entire length and built to a higher standard to withstand considerably heavier lorry traffic. Financial assistance was obtained from a number of Western sources, particularly the United States and the World Bank, and the project was carried out by Western contractors. The Zambian section of the Great North Road was completed in 1970, with the Tanzanian stretch finished two years later, and total costs — almost £50 million — were considerably higher than originally estimated. By then, the Tanzanian *Daily News* pointed out, 'Hell Run' had become the 'Paradise Expressway'.[13]

Zambia-Tanzania Road Services was established in May 1966 to haul goods between Dar es Salaam and the Copperbelt. The two governments, each owning 35 per cent of the shares in the company, went into partnership with the Italian firm of Intersomer, a subsidiary of the Fiat company, which supplied the trucks. It is the largest road transport company in Africa, with a fleet of 600 lorries, and cargo handled rose to 479,000 tons by 1973. Italian commercial firms have succeeded in filling a number of the new commercial gaps created by the reorientation of Zambia's transport links. They not only participated in the Road Services, but also built the oil pipeline, constructed part of the Zambian section of the Great North Road, and managed Zambia Airways.

During the UDI emergency, several other routes to Tanzanian ports were briefly used. The Tanzanian Central Line, running from Dar es Salaam to Lake Tanganyika, offered a number of possibilities. Some traffic was sent from Zambia (via the Congolese railway system) to the Lake Tanganyika port of Kalémié, or by road to the Zambian port of Mpulungu, and then by barge to Kigoma. The Great North Road could also be used to carry freight to the Tanzanian border and a dirt track ran northwards to the East African Railways branch line at Mpanda. Those three routes were used experimentally during 1966–7, but none of them proved economic.

The port of Mtwara, in southern Tanzania, also handled Zambian traffic for several years after UDI. Mtwara, with its excellent natural harbour, had originally been developed after World War II as part of the notorious Groundnut Scheme, which squandered £36 million on an unsuccessful project to raise agricultural production. A railway line had been built from Mtwara to Nachingwea in 1952 but, after large losses had accumulated, it was closed down ten years later. During the early 1960s there had been some discussion of building a railway from Mtwara to Lake Nyasa, to serve Malawi, and possibly extending the line to the Copperbelt. In the end, however, Malawi decided to proceed with a rail link through Mozambique to the port of Nacala, rather than develop a much longer transport route through independent Africa to Mtwara.

Kaunda visited Mtwara in May 1966 and expressed interest in developing the port as an outlet for Zambian traffic. Mtwara only handled a very small proportion of Tanzania's foreign trade, so consideration was given to turning over the port for exclusive Zambian use. It would, however, have cost at least £15 million to improve the road to the Zambian border. The Tanzanian government might also have been reluctant to lease the harbour to a foreign power, even a friendly regime. Mtwara was situated dangerously close to Mozambique, just twenty miles north of the border, so the port would have been under constant threat of attack from Portuguese forces. Zambia probably felt that it was safer to be dependent on a port which Tanzania shared a vital interest in improving, rather than relying on one which was only of marginal concern to the Tanzanian government. Small amounts of Zambian cargo were airfreighted into Mtwara, and some traffic sent by road during 1966 and 1967, so the southern Tanzanian port temporarily became a useful outlet for landlocked Zambia.

Between 1966 and 1968, some Zambian cargo was also sent through Malawi to ports in Mozambique. The Great East Road, unsurfaced until 1969, runs from Lusaka to the Malawi border and there is then a short stretch, which still remains untarred, to the Malawian railway at Salima or Balaka. The railway connects with the Mozambican port of Beira and, since the completion of a rail link in 1970, to the excellent new harbour at Nacala.

The route through Malawi had a number of serious drawbacks: it required trans-shipment from road to rail, the capacity of the Malawian railway system was insufficient to handle much Zambian traffic, and it involved dependence on both Malawi and Mozambique. The dangers of using transport routes through the Portuguese territories have already been outlined, but relations between Zambia and Malawi were also tense during the late 1960s. After a split in the Malawian government in later 1964 several Cabinet Ministers had fled to Lusaka. President Banda had also made vague territorial claims to the Eastern Province of Zambia in September 1968. Zambia, on its side, was suspicious of Malawi's conciliatory attitude towards the minority regimes of Southern Africa. For both economic and political reasons the Zambian government was therefore reluctant to invest in the development of alternative transport routes through Malawi to ports in Mozambique.

There were two elements in Zambia's search for reliable outlets for its foreign trade. The first was *disengagement* from dependence on its traditional route through Rhodesia. The dangers of relying on this outlet had been shown by the numerous disruptions that occurred and the wisdom of developing alternative routes was confirmed by Smith's decision to close his border with Zambia in January 1973. By this time Zambia was in a sufficiently strong position to resist Rhodesia's threats.

Secondly, Zambia embarked on a programme of *diversification* away from a single route so that the country would never again be so vulnerable to economic and political pressures from those who controlled its transport routes. Diversification was initially a necessity in the UDI emergency and during 1966 and 1967 over a dozen routes were used. Most of them proved expensive, adding greatly to Zambia's transport bill, and few had the capacity to handle a significant proportion of the country's foreign trade. All routes, with the exception of those through Tanzania, were for one reason or another politically unacceptable, except as short-term emergency measures, so Kaunda had little choice but to concentrate new investment on the development of links to Dar es Salaam.

UDI acted as a catalyst in encouraging the Zambian government to search for alternative routes. In the short term the UDI emergency diverted the attention of Zambian planners away from the Tanzam railway — which, it was assumed, could hardly be open for traffic in under a decade — to the immediate problems of transporting the country's foreign trade. But the Zambian government became even more committed to the proposed line to Dar es Salaam as the ultimate solution. Only a railway to Tanzania could break Rhodesia's hold over Zambia and provide a reliable route with the capacity to handle the country's foreign trade at an economic cost. The difficulty was to find a foreign donor willing to finance this enormous project.

# III
# SEARCH FOR ASSISTANCE

The Tanzam railway represented a symbol of the aspirations of independent Zambia and Tanzania. But the contradiction remained that it could only be built with financial and technical assistance from abroad. Kaunda and Nyerere probably first discussed the proposed rail link between their countries early in 1961. The Zambian leader was then preoccupied with the immediate problem of winning independence, so it was only after the British government announced the dissolution of the Central African Federation, in March 1963, that attention could be focused on the Tanzam project. Simon Kapwepwe, Kaunda's closest confidant, was sent to Dar es Salaam for discussions and Nyerere responded favourably to the proposal for a railway between Dar es Salaam and the Copperbelt.

Kaunda and Nyerere began the long search for external funds to build the rail link. Requests went out to all major aid donors, both governments and multilateral financial institutions, while a number of large foreign companies also considered the project. The result was a series of studies and surveys of the proposed railway, numerous enough to fill a whole bookshelf, but a lack of firm offers. Strong forces opposed the Tanzam link and they were, ironically, led by some of the political and commercial interests which owed their existence to Cecil Rhodes and his Chartered Company. In the end there was no Western offer to complete the imperial dream on terms acceptable to the African nationalists. Only China was willing to help fill the longest gap in the Cape-to-Cairo route.

## LONRHO AND THE IMPERIAL DREAM

Almost a century after Cecil Rhodes had proposed a Cape-to-Cairo railway it seemed that the most likely candidate to complete the project would be the British company of Lonrho. Most European firms operating in Africa had feared the 'winds of change' that swept the continent during the early 1960s. But Lonrho—its name a shortened form of the *Lon*don and *Rho*desian Mining and Land Company—saw a new opportunity for expanding its commercial interests northwards into black Africa. A decade later, in 1973, a boardroom row over the firm's 'adventuristic' policies in Africa splashed Lonrho's name across the British press. But the company's hopes in independent Africa were rewarded as profits soared from £½ million in 1963 to £46 million ten years later.

By the 1960s three stretches remained to be built in the projected Cape-to-Cairo railway and it is curious that Lonrho has expressed interest in all three projects. The Egyptian rail system continues south from Cairo to the Aswan High Dam and it is separated from the Sudanese railway by a 300-mile gap down the Nile Valley. From Wadi Halfa, on the Sudanese border, the railway winds its way southwards through Khartoum to the southern Sudanese town of Wau. Then 500 miles remains before the Ugandan rail system is reached at Pakwach, on the Nile. Lonrho, which has recently spread its interests into the Arab world, saw north-eastern Africa as an important bridge and Tiny Rowland, the company's boss, revealed in 1973 that 'we have an option to link the Egyptian and Sudanese railway systems . . . we would like to link Sudan's railways with the East African systems'.[1] It is possible that Lonrho, stepping into the footsteps of Lord Kitchener, may one day bring the tracks down from Cairo as far as Dar es Salaam.

The final gap in the Cape-to-Cairo line, the stretch from Dar es Salaam to the Copperbelt, had seemed an ideal project to launch Lonrho's jump northwards into independent Africa back in the early 1960s. A preliminary survey of the project, based on the Gibb report of 1952, was prepared by the company for the government of Northern Rhodesia in November 1963. Construction costs of laying the track from the Copperbelt to the Tanganyikan border were estimated at £17 million.

Lonrho offered to put up the capital, as well as to operate the line, with the crucial condition that the new railway would be given a concession to carry all of Northern Rhodesia's copper exports. But Kaunda's government was reluctant to give Lonrho a monopoly of the country's copper traffic. First, it would have made the nation completely dependent on a single route to the coast and this had been one of the reasons why the government had decided to build an alternative line. Secondly, Northern Rhodesia had a joint share in Rhodesia Railways, which was naturally strongly opposed to the construction of a rival line to Dar es Salaam, and the government would have had to compensate RR if traffic had been sent on other routes.

In December 1963 the two Rhodesias had signed an agreement under which they undertook to compensate RR if either of them diverted traffic on to another railway. Southern Rhodesia had no reason to develop an alternative to the traditional route into Mozambique. Since the restriction therefore only applied in practice to Northern Rhodesia, the agreement rightly came to be regarded as an 'unequal treaty' tying Zambia to its southern neighbour. If Northern Rhodesia had given Lonrho the monopoly of carrying all its copper production, running at around 600,000 tons a year, then up to £5 million a year compensation would have to have been paid to RR on exports alone.

In view of Lonrho's demand for monopoly rights to transport all Northern Rhodesia's copper, as well as the difficulty of securing funds to build the Tanganyikan section of the line, the company's offer was turned down. Lonrho continued to look for new transport projects in Central Africa, while the Tanganyikan and Northern Rhodesian governments went on with the search for foreign assistance to build their rail link.

## EAST AFRICA LOOKS AGAIN

When Lonrho offered to build and operate the Northern Rhodesian section of the railway it had been assumed that East African Railways (EAR) would be responsible for continuing the line on the Tanganyikan side. The nearest railhead in Tanganyika was the branch to Mikumi, running south from the Kilosa junction on the Central Line, which had been completed in 1960 to tap road traffic from the Southern Highlands. Four years later the railway was continued southwards to serve the Kilombero Sugar Estate at Kidatu. A preliminary study had considered extending the line down the Kilombero Valley, possibly as far as Makumbako, but the cost of this 250 mile section would have been over £12 million. With the growing determination of the Zambian and Tanzanian leaders to proceed with a rail link between Dar es Salaam and the Copperbelt, plans to extend the EAR line were shelved.

In December 1963, following a request from the Tanganyikan government, EAR updated the 1952 Gibb report on the Tanzam project. Total costs of the line, including rolling stock and interest on the loan, had risen to £51 million. It was assumed that the Tanzam line would not carry copper exports then being sent via Rhodesia Railways, but rather that the new route would only take the expected increase in copper production — estimated at 250,000 tons by

1975 — in order to avoid compensating RR. By 1975, claimed EAR, the proposed rail link could be earning a yearly surplus of £½ million.

The Tanzanian government was determined to proceed with the Tanzam project. But East African Railways, despite the favourable conclusions of their report, showed relatively little interest in the link. Kenya and Uganda, the other members of EAR, were reluctant to become involved in the line to Zambia. First of all a huge investment would have been required — a larger amount than the total spent on the region's railways since 1945 — so it was felt that other rail projects in Kenya and Uganda might have had to have been postponed. Secondly, neither of the other two East African states had much to gain economically from the proposed line. Uganda had virtually no economic ties with Zambia. Kenya's industrial development was dependent on the Tanzanian market, so it was reluctant to see its southern trading partner reorientate its economic links towards Zambia.

There were serious tensions over economic co-operation in East Africa at this time, particularly between Tanzania and Kenya, so in this strained atmosphere there was less sympathy than there might otherwise have been for Tanzania's interests. On the other hand, Kenya was reluctant to go so far as to veto the Tanzam project because this might have jeopardized the existence of the East African common market. Kenya and Uganda, despite their lack of enthusiasm, did not stand in the way of Tanzania's wish to build a link to Zambia.

At the beginning of October 1964, just three weeks before Zambia's independence, Kaunda and the three East African leaders met at Dar es Salaam and took the historic decision to proceed with the railway. Further talks in March 1965 led to the establishment of the Zambia-East Africa Inter-Governmental Ministerial Committee to seek foreign assistance for building the line. Tanzania and Zambia were empowered to begin initial soundings to potential donors for their own sections of the route.

## WASHINGTON APPROACHED

A team of World Bank experts arrived in Lusaka just as the Lonrho team was leaving. The World Bank, a multilateral financial institution, had been asked by the Northern Rhodesian government to examine the proposed rail link to Dar es Salaam in 1963. Its report, submitted in May 1964, came out strongly against the project but, as Nyerere later pointed out, it had been 'given terms of reference which virtually pre-judged the issue'.[2]

The World Bank, since it normally lends money on conventional banking terms, ignored the political aspect of the project, and, in particular, Northern Rhodesia's wish to reduce its dependence on the white South. One blatant illustration of the Bank's failure to consider political factors was its assumption that trade between South Africa and the three East African countries would run at 18,000 tons a year. TANU had in fact banned trade with South Africa as far back as 1960 and, just a few months before the World Bank began its survey, the newly-established Organization of African Unity (OAU) had called for a boycott of commerce with South Africa. Nyerere and Kaunda felt that the World Bank was out of touch with the political realities and aspirations of independent Africa.

The World Bank came out strongly against the railway to Dar es Salaam because it assumed that the line would only carry goods between Central and East Africa, with the bulk of Zambia's foreign trade being transported on existing routes to ports in Mozambique and Angola. This analysis was based on two assumptions which were later found to be invalid.

First, the Bank report stated that there was an ample spare capacity on existing railways for at least ten to twenty years. But with the increase in Zambian imports after independence, the growing volume of trade in Central Africa would have required substantial investment in the Rhodesian and Portuguese railway systems. It was later suggested, in the Anglo-Canadian report on the project prepared two years later, that these improvements — costing £84 million — would have been almost as expensive as building a new line to Dar es Salaam.

Secondly, the World Bank assumed that operating costs on the Tanzam railway would be high. Because of the gradients involved (with the line climbing up to nearly 6,000 feet) and the different gauges in East and Central Africa (with the need for trans-shipment), it was estimated that operating costs on the Tanzam railway would be higher than on the routes to Mozambique and Angola. This conclusion was later disputed by the Anglo-Canadian survey which suggested that the Tanzam line could be run more economically than either the RR or the Benguela routes.

Since the World Bank assumed that there was ample capacity for Zambia's traffic on existing routes and that operating costs on the proposed Tanzam line would be higher, it estimated that even by 1980 the line would be carrying only 87,000 tons of traffic between

Zambia and Tanzania. The Bank recommended that the need for transport facilities for this volume of traffic 'could be met very much more cheaply by improving existing roads than by building the new railroad'.[3] A railway would cost an estimated £58 million and, it was claimed, would run at a loss until after 1990. Improving the Great North Road, on the other hand, would involve an expenditure of only £8 million and, along with a series of feeder roads, would provide a more flexible means of transport.

The World Bank not only turned down the request to finance the Tanzam railway, but also made it almost impossible for East African Railways to participate in the project. A clause inserted in a Bank loan agreement with EAR in September 1965 prohibited the Railways from undertaking any new investment which might jeopardize their ability to meet loan repayments to the Bank. Some observers speculated that the Bank was primarily interested in protecting its existing investments in the Rhodesian line to Mozambique.

The World Bank report touched off the 'road versus rail' controversy. Tanzania and Zambia were determined to have a rail link and there was a feeling that a road represented a somewhat inferior form of transport. Railways also require less maintenance and spare parts, compared with truck haulage, and this reduces dependence on external sources. The crucial issue, however, was the amount of Zambian traffic that would have been sent through Dar es Salaam. A road would only have had the capacity to handle a small part of Zambia's foreign trade, and operating costs by truck would have been higher than by rail.

A study of future traffic levels on the Great North Road, prepared by the Stanford Research Institute and financed by USAID, was conducted in 1966. It concluded that an improved road 'would be complementary to a future railroad, should one be built, since it would provide feeder service to the railroad and facilitate development of new areas'. It is true that the Tanzam railway runs parallel to the Great North Road for about 40 per cent of the distance. But for the remainder of the route the road and rail links serve different areas. Most important of all, the road would not compete with the rail link because 'the railroad would undoubtedly be more economical for copper traffic'.[4] And, in addition, only a railway would have made it feasible to exploit the rich mineral deposits in south-west Tanzania.

Tanzania and Zambia, although they were determined to build a rail link, also needed external assistance to improve the Great North

Road. By 1966, it was clear that it would not be easy to secure an acceptable offer to finance the Tanzam railway and that, in any case, it would not be operational until the 1970s. Meanwhile UDI, and the imposition of sanctions against the rebel regime, made Zambia's dependence on its traditional transport route increasingly dangerous. An improvement of the road outlet to Dar es Salaam was essential as a short-term measure before the proposed railway became operational.

The World Bank had suggested that the Great North Road could be upgraded for £8 million, with part of the route left untarred, but because the route now had to be designed for a much greater volume of traffic than originally envisaged, total costs in the end exceeded £50 million. Since much of this was financed by the World Bank and the United States, it is possible that these donors were partly motivated by a perceived need to compete with Chinese assistance in building the railway.

The negative conclusions of the World Bank survey of the Tanzam railway were echoed by a number of other studies. A United Nations mission, which prepared a report on the Northern Rhodesian economy in March 1964, commented that if plans for the project went ahead, there was 'a risk of an expensive mistake'.[5] NEDCO, a Dutch firm of consultants employed by the World Bank in 1964 to prepare a survey of Zambia's transport needs, also came out against the proposed rail link. An American study on transport in Central Africa, financed by USAID and prepared in 1965 by the Brookings Institution in Washington, commented somewhat cryptically that the Tanzam railway 'can find no justification except in "unreal" definitions . . . . The economics of the rail link are clearly not persuasive. What remains are political issues which are often clothed in economic dress.'[6] Tanzania and Zambia, on the other hand, felt that the situation was the reverse: Western studies rejected the project for political reasons and disguised their rejection in economic terms.

An official request for assistance with the Tanzam railway had been submitted to the United States in May 1965. The American reaction was very similar to that of the World Bank. Since the United States provides a third of the organization's funds and the bank had its headquarters in Washington, it seemed that the World Bank had all along been reflecting American views on the Tanzam project.

The Tanzanian and Zambian request was viewed in rather a different light in the United States after Nyerere's announcement in June 1965 that the Chinese had put forward an offer. This immediately provoked a flurry of diplomatic activity. Wayne

Fredericks, the American State Department's African specialist, flew straight to London—where Nyerere and Kaunda were attending the Commonwealth summit conference—for consultations with the two African leaders. When the Tanzanian President returned to Dar es Salaam, he caustically complained that Western representatives had spent more time seeking details of the Chinese offer than they had in discussing his request for assistance.

Fredericks offered United States finance for yet another survey of the railway—on condition the study also considered the advantages of an improved road route—but the offer was never taken up. The American State Department's Bureau of African Affairs apparently felt that the Tanzanian and Zambian request for assistance should be seriously considered. Other officials, including Secretary of State Dean Rusk and President Lyndon Johnson, were firmly against the project and their views won the day.

In Washington there was a growing feeling that foreign aid did not provide the returns which had originally been expected and there was a general disillusionment with the turn of events in Africa. The Americans were particularly critical of the political situation in Tanzania. Events in Zanzibar, described as the 'Cuba of Africa' after the January 1964 revolution, were misinterpreted as a slide towards communism. The development of Tanzanian relations with China, including active consideration of the Chinese offer to build the Tanzam line, antagonized the United States. 'The West which doesn't want to build the railway', Nyerere once commented, 'doesn't want the Chinese to build it either.'[7] Peking's interest in the Tanzam line might have driven the United States to make an offer to prevent the Chinese from moving into East Africa. But Washington soon took the view that talk of Chinese assistance was merely a bluff to blackmail the West into funding the railway.

The request for United States aid for the railway certainly came at an inauspicious time, when Tanzanian-American relations were at their lowest ebb. In November 1964 and January 1965 Tanzania had accused the Americans of involvement in plots to overthrow Nyerere's government. Although both accusations later turned out to be based on false evidence, they led to a deterioration in Tanzanian-United States relations and the withdrawal of their ambassadors.

The Tanzanian government was also becoming increasingly suspicious of American activities in the Third World. The United States was seen as supporting the *status quo* in Southern Africa and NATO was certainly a major supplier of arms to Portugal. The

Stanleyville incident, in which United States planes were used to land
Belgian paratroops in the Congo to rescue white hostages, angered
Nyerere. Growing American intervention in Vietnam was strongly
criticized by the Tanzanian government. The war in South East Asia
demonstrated America's willingness to spend its vast resources in the
Third World and made the refusal to finance the Tanzam even
more galling: 'Our railroad', a senior Tanzanian official pointed
out in 1967, 'could be built for what the Americans are spending in
Vietnam every four days.'[8]

American officials, assuming that their experience was of universal
validity, pointed out that they had spent the last twenty-five years
pulling up rail lines which had become uneconomic. Tanzania and
Zambia replied that railways had opened up the American West in
the earlier era. No Western government offered to finance the
Tanzam line. But what angered Nyerere and Kaunda was America's
response that the railway was totally unnecessary and that an
improved road, which could only handle a much smaller volume of
traffic, would be sufficient for Zambia's needs.

## APPEAL TO BRITAIN

Britain, because of its colonial connection with Tanzania and
Zambia, was one of the first Western countries approached to finance
the Tanzam railway. In May 1963, during one of Kaunda's visits to
London, the need for a rail link to Dar es Salaam was discussed with
Rab Butler, Britain's Secretary of State. When Barbara Castle, UK
Minister for Overseas Development, visited Dar es Salaam and
Lusaka two years later, the project was raised again, but the
Tanzanian and Zambian leaders were told that the British balance of
payments crisis precluded further aid commitments to Africa.

Nyerere's announcement of the Chinese offer at the
Commonwealth Summit in June 1965 brought the British
government into action. Barbara Castle met with the Tanzanian and
Zambian Presidents, who were an hour late in joining their
Commonwealth colleagues in Marlborough House, and they returned
with yet another offer of a survey of the railway. Britain's offer, which
was dependent on the contract being awarded to a British firm, only
covered half the costs of the £150,000 survey. The financing of the
other half caused serious diplomatic problems. Britain refused to
provide the full amount for fear that this would be seen as a
precedent for the funding of the railway itself, and, moreover, it was
felt that Zambia could raise the other half if it was serious about the

project. Tanzania, however, refused to contribute on the grounds that China had offered to undertake a free study of the Tanzanian section of the line. Zambia, too, was worried about setting a precedent for the financing of the actual railway, so the Zambian government was reluctant to provide the remaining half of the survey costs.

The deadlock was resolved by Canadian Prime Minister, Lester Pearson, who offered to put up the rest of the money. Canada, a fellow member of the Commonwealth, had good relations with the two African nations, and was also considered as a possible participant in an international consortium to build the Tanzam line. The Canadians have had a great deal of experience in railway engineering. Although in fact they did not contribute towards the building of the Tanzam project, they have provided aid for the railway systems in the two African countries. A £1-million programme of managerial assistance to reorganize ZR was begun in 1970 and five years later a similar arrangement was made with EAR. During the 1970s loans of £6 million to EAR and £2½ million to ZR have been provided to purchase Canadian rolling stock.

In September 1965 it was announced that the Anglo-Canadian survey would be prepared by Maxwell Stamp Associates. This British firm of consultants had already established a good reputation with the Zambian government over the affair of Chartered Consolidated's claims to mineral royalties. On the eve of Zambian independence Chartered Consolidated had demanded £50 million in compensation for giving up its lucrative mineral royalties, but – after a Maxwell Stamp study had exposed the weakness of Chartered's case – the company accepted a token payment of £2 million just a matter of hours before independence.

The formal agreement setting up the Anglo-Canadian survey was signed on 13 November, two days after Ian Smith's proclamation of UDI had made Zambia's need for new transport links more urgent, and a few days later a survey team arrived in Lusaka. Maxwell Stamp Associates were responsible for preparing the report, a thorough engineering and economic survey of the project, with the assistance of two British firms – Livesey and Henderson (consulting engineers) and Sumpton Berkeley (economic advisers) – and Canadian Aero-Surveys.

The Anglo-Canadian survey, completed in nine months, was the most detailed study of the Tanzam railway that had been prepared since 1952 and it took the project right on to the design stage. The report concluded that the line was 'a feasible and economic proposition'.[9] The railway could be built for £126 million and should produce an annual surplus of £11 million by 1971. The previous World Bank report, completed only two years before, had stated that the line would cost only £51 million, but that it still would not be economically viable. Why the apprent discrepancy between the two studies?

There were three main reasons why the capital costs had more than doubled. First, new survey techniques, such as aerial photography, clearly revealed the extremely difficult engineering problems involved in crossing the Rift Valley section of the line in southern Tanzania. Secondly, the estimated costs of rolling stock leapt up from £3 million to £26 million in order to cope with the much larger volume of traffic which the Anglo-Canadian study envisaged (more than nineteen times the World Bank's forecast). Finally, inflation raised total costs during the two years between the surveys.

The Anglo-Canadian study, unlike that of the World Bank, assumed that all Zambia's copper exports would be sent on the Tanzam route to Dar es Salaam. Total traffic available to the new line was therefore estimated at 3,134,000 ton-miles in 1971 — compared with the much lower Bank figure of 168,000 ton-miles by 1975. The changing political situation in Central Africa, particularly the effects of UDI and the imminent break-up of Rhodesia Railways, meant that Zambia could now plan to export its copper through Dar es Salaam without paying compensation to RR. The Anglo-Canadian survey also pointed out that Rhodesia Railways had recently operated at full capacity because of the rising level of Zambian trade. If the Tanzam line was not built, then additional investment would have had to be made to increase the capacity of the Rhodesian railway route and this would have cost the surprisingly high figure of £84 million.

The Anglo-Canadian report suggested that the Tanzam line would be an 'ideal railway operation' since 90 per cent of the traffic would be cargo carried between the Copperbelt and the port of Dar es Salaam.[10] Through-running trains carrying end-to-end traffic would reduce running costs, which would be .35 pence per ton-mile, compared with .48 pence on RR. Cheaper costs, in conjunction with Zambia's stated policy of reducing its ties with the white South, should ensure that virtually all Zambian overseas trade — estimated to reach 4.3 million tons by 1981 — was sent via Dar es Salaam. The Tanzam line should be economically viable and its operating surplus would repay the capital cost of the project within thirteen years. It would also have the advantage of reducing Zambia's 'dangerous dependence on Southern Rhodesia'.[11]

By the time the Anglo-Canadian survey was completed, in August 1966, Western interest in its results had waned. In January 1967 US-AID commissioned an American firm of consultants, ARENCO, to evaluate the Anglo-Canadian survey. The consultants' report concluded that the study 'does not provide an adequate basis for determining the engineering/economic feasibility of the project'.[12] But the United States, in any case, had already rejected the Tanzanian and Zambian request.

It seemed that the British decision to finance the Anglo-Canadian survey may have been partly a tactic to gain time, in the hope of delaying Tanzanian and Zambian acceptance of the Chinese offer. Despite the fact that Britain and Canada had financed the survey, it appears that copies of the report were not officially sent to the two Western governments. It is true that Canada, even if she had wanted to participate in the building of the railway, could only have afforded to have put up a small part of the capital. Financial considerations, particularly a deteriorating balance of payments situation, were also partly responsible for Britain's decision to turn down the request for assistance. But just as it was mainly for political reasons that the two African countries wanted the railway, so it was also largely political factors that were behind Britain's rejection of the project.

The British government's attitude towards minority rule in Southern Africa, and particularly its weak response to UDI, angered Tanzania and Zambia. A few weeks after UDI the Organization of African Unity passed a resolution calling on members to break off diplomatic relations with Britain if the rebellion was not crushed by 15 December 1965. Kaunda never actually cut diplomatic links, primarily because of Zambia's need for British assistance in imposing sanctions against Rhodesia, but ties between Lusaka and London became very strained. Tensions reached new heights in 1967 when the Zambian ambassador in Dar es Salaam, who had just been appointed to London, caused a diplomatic incident by calling Britain 'a humbled toothless bulldog'.[13]

Tanzania became the first Commonwealth member ever to break off diplomatic relations with Britain. The Union Jack was hauled down from the High Commission in the centre of Dar es Salaam and, after Canada had agreed to act as a diplomatic intermediary, it was replaced by the Canadian flag. In the end only eight other OAU members actually implemented the organization's resolution. Tanzania, however, was the only African state to suffer financially when a British loan of £7½ million, promised for the country's First Five Year Plan, was frozen after the break.

Although the request for assistance with the Tanzam project came from the Zambia-East Africa Inter-Governmental Ministerial Committee, rather than from the Tanzanian government, widespread African criticism of British policies over Rhodesia made London unresponsive. If Britain had helped in this way to free Zambia from the shackles of the white South, her failure to defeat Smith might have caused less bitterness. But the British government probably saw it as too expensive a way of making up for lost prestige.

## LAST REQUESTS

The United States and Britain were the two Western nations most likely to consider financing the Tanzam railway. The Inter-Governmental Ministerial Committee also submitted requests to West Germany, France, and Japan, while less formal approaches were made to a number of other potential donors. But no Western aid was forthcoming.

The request to West Germany was submitted early in 1965, but that country's relations with Tanzania had reached a low ebb. Until 1964 Tanganyika maintained good links with Bonn. But Zanzibar, on the other hand, became the first non-communist country to grant full diplomatic recognition to East Germany. The union of Tanganyika and Zanzibar in April 1964 presented Nyerere with a dilemma that was not resolved until the following February. It was then announced that Tanzania would maintain full diplomatic relations with West Germany, with the East German government permitted to open a consulate in Dar es Salaam on the understanding that this was not interpreted as official recognition. West Germany, in accordance with the Hallstein Doctrine, reacted angrily to an East German presence in Dar es Salaam and immediately withdrew military aid from Tanzania. Bonn also made it clear that economic assistance was under review and Nyerere, refusing to be threatened, reacted by asking that all West German government assistance — £4 million of loans and £3 million of technical assistance — should be withdrawn. In this atmosphere West Germany was unlikely to give serious consideration to the Tanzam railway and the Tanzanians would, in any case, have been reluctant to accept West German aid.

France was also approached for assistance. But the French government showed very little interest in the project. France has always concentrated her foreign aid on the former French-ruled territories and has provided little assistance to the Anglophone African nations. It appears that no other European countries were approached. This was presumably because of the large cost of the project compared with the aid programme of potential donors, but it is perhaps somewhat surprising that requests were not submitted to the Scandinavian countries.

Japan, at least during the mid-1960s, had only just begun to cultivate relations with Africa. But Japanese commercial concerns were interested in the railway. Businessmen in Tokyo, searching for new markets for their growing steel exports, saw the thousand miles of track to the Copperbelt as a golden opportunity. Japan concentrated on wooing Zambia and, after a visit to Tokyo by two Zambian Ministers, a Japanese mission in Lusaka made an offer of a free survey of the rail link. This offer was never taken up.

Japan did not become directly involved in the Tanzam project—although sales of steel and earth-moving equipment to China increased to provide supplies for the railway—but the Japanese have taken part in several other rail projects in the two African countries. In 1970 a Japanese firm produced a feasibility study of a rail line between Arusha and the Lake Victoria port of Musoma and in 1972 the Japanese government provided Zambia with a loan to purchase rolling stock and equipment for ZR.

An approach for Soviet assistance had been made relatively early, with the project included in the 'shopping list' of requests which Tanzanian Vice-President Rashidi Kawawa carried to Moscow in August 1964, and Nyerere apparently made a further appeal to the Soviet Union the following year. A Tanzanian memorandum submitted to Moscow pointed out that although the World Bank, a Western-dominated institution which the Russians regarded with suspicion, had rejected the proposal, 'the rail link scheme has an economic and strategic importance for the continent as a whole'.[14]

It is somewhat surprising that the Soviet Union did not consider the Tanzam project more seriously. Its interest in this strategically important part of Africa has been demonstrated by the amount of Soviet military assistance provided to the liberation movements struggling against minority rule. The possibility of Chinese assistance with the Tanzam railway might have encouraged the Soviet Union to make a counter-offer in order to prevent its rival from gaining influence in an important Third World arena. Soviet development aid to Africa—if we omit Egypt—has, however, remained at a relatively low level. Between 1959 and 1973 total aid actually disbursed was around £165 million. This amount is just under the cost of the Tanzam project. The Soviet Union, it is true, did finance the Aswan Dam, but the Russians were probably wary about embarking on another project of a similar magnitude.

In view of the enormous cost of the railway, and the reluctance of Western governments to finance the project, there was some discussion of forming an international consortium. This could have consisted of governments, multilateral finance institutions, international companies, or a combination of these groups. It was suggested that the African Development Bank, which had just been established by the UN Economic Commission for Africa, would be a suitable body to co-ordinate the consortium.

An African Development Bank consortium would have had a number of advantages for Tanzania and Zambia over bilateral assistance from the West. First, a consortium loan appeared to preserve the non-aligned position of Tanzania and Zambia; and, secondly, the channelling of funds through the Development Bank might have given the African countries slightly more control over the scheme. A consortium answered the Western governments' claims that the railway was too expensive for any of them to finance alone, but it made the project less appealing to them since it would have reduced the influence that individual donors could have exerted over Tanzania and Zambia.

A formal request to the Development Bank was submitted by the Inter-Governmental Ministerial Committee in February 1966, as soon as the Bank became operational, and two studies were commissioned for the project. These were a soil survey of the most difficult section of the route, from Makumbako to Chita, and a study of the expansion of Dar es Salaam port that would be necessary to handle the railway's traffic. The African Development Bank, with its relatively small resources, could not have provided more than £10 million, so the problem of securing the necessary funds would have basically remained unresolved. The request to the Bank was, in any case, overtaken by events when the Chinese offer was finally accepted.

A number of multinational companies, which were interested in either constructing the line or supplying equipment, pressed for the project to go ahead. One such firm was Kaiser International, an American company, which apparently offered to build the line in August 1965. Their assessment of the railway was that it would have been 'highly profitable' and 'one of the most financially attractive ventures in Africa'.[15] The senior official in Kaiser International dealing with the project later claimed that he had 'always suspected that President Johnson may have telephoned' Mr Kaiser to ask him to drop the project because of pressure from Britain.[16] Nothing, in the end, ever came of Kaiser International's interest in the railway.

A group of seven multinational companies was reported in 1967 to have attempted to organize a consortium to build the Tanzam line. By this time, however, Western financial circles were becoming increasingly apprehensive about the direction of Tanzanian policy, particularly after the nationalizations following the Arusha Declaration in January 1967, and they were wary of making further investment in the country. The Tanzanian and Zambian governments also became increasingly suspicious of offers which suddenly appeared after the project had been rejected by Western governments. It all seemed to be 'part and parcel of the delaying tactics', the Tanzanian Transport Minister remarked, to ensure that the Chinese offer was not taken up.[17]

## WESTERN REFUSAL

Nyerere told Chou En-lai that the West had 'assured us that the railway was uneconomic and unnecessary—as indeed it was from their point of view'. A line linking Tanzania and Zambia 'would take traffic from the railways built by, and run for the benefit of, the imperialist forces' and 'it would strengthen the economies and the security of both our anti-imperialist states'.[18]

Entrenched political and economic interests in Southern Africa were generally opposed to the building of the Tanzam line. By far the most important user of Zambia's transport routes to the sea are the two giant copper companies—Anglo-American (despite its name owned by a South African company) and Roan Consolidated Mines (mainly controlled by United States shareholders)—which not only provide almost all Zambia's exports, but also import large quantities of fuel (particularly coal and oil), machinery, and other goods to operate the mines.

The main concern of the two mining companies has been that cheap and reliable routes should be available to coastal ports. Along with the copper consumers, they have therefore feared the political uncertainty that followed UDI and the subsequent disruptions to Zambia's transport outlets. Anglo-American, since its massive financial interests are mainly concentrated in South Africa, opposed Zambia's break with the white South. The company also owns the Wankie colliery in Rhodesia, which supplied a million tons of coal to

Zambia, and this valuable market was cut off after UDI with Zambia's decision to develop domestic deposits. The copper companies have not encouraged Zambia's attempt to reduce its dependence on RR. But, on the other hand, they decided not to oppose the project actively because of their need to retain the goodwill of the Zambian government.

Tanganyika Concessions, another major company operating in Southern Africa, was also against the Tanzam project because it would have diverted Zambian traffic away from the rail line to Lobito. The company, largely controlled by British shareholders, owns 90 per cent of the shares of Benguela Railways, and is believed to have put pressure on the British government to oppose the building of the Tanzam line. Tanganyika Concessions also proposed the construction of a direct rail link between Zambia and Angola in order to discourage the Zambian government from proceeding with the Tanzam project. 'The world has never seen such a proliferation of railway projects which are now being canvassed,' Nyerere remarked in a discussion of the Tanzam line in 1969, and 'all of them are designed to try and stop this railway from being built.'[19]

The interests of companies like Anglo-American and Tanganyika Concessions, along with many other firms operating in Zambia which were subsidiaries of companies based in South Africa, were closely aligned to the concerns of the South African and Portuguese governments. Tanganyika Concessions' links with Portugal, for example, can be discerned from the directors' remarks in their 1969 report. Prime Minister Caetano had just visited Angola and 'it was natural', the directors pointed out, 'for the Chairman of the Board of your great undertaking, which is, by definition, devoted to the public service, to wish to be present on such a memorable occasion'. The fortunate Chairman was even invited to fly back to Lisbon in the presidential plane, a gesture which, 'despite an old personal friendship' with Caetano, deeply touched the Chairman.[20]

The minority regimes of Southern Africa were strongly opposed to the Tanzam line for both economic and political reasons. A new line diverting Zambian traffic from Beira and Lobito would have taken away profitable transit revenue from the two ports. The state-owned Mozambique Railways and the line to Lobito, controlled by Tanganyika Concessions, would also have been affected. Rhodesia Railways' dependence on Zambian traffic was shown by the losses of almost £1 million a month which piled up after Smith closed the border between the two countries in January 1973. Zambia was a lucrative market for South African and Rhodesian exporters, so the reorientation of economic links northwards — of which the building of the Tanzam link was an important element — would have disrupted this valuable trade. In addition, as long as Zambia relied on its traditional route through Rhodesia and Mozambique, the minority regimes retained a means of applying pressure on the Zambian government to reduce its support to the liberation movements.

It is difficult to determine the extent of the influence of Southern African interests over Western governments and institutions that were approached to fund the railway. The West displayed relatively little concern with the liberation struggle and, at least in the economic sphere, white domination in Southern Africa may well have served their short-term interests. Western governments therefore saw little need to finance a railway whose primary purpose was to reduce Zambian dependence on the white South.

Other powerful lobbies in the West were opposed to the Tanzam railway. The Zambian Vice-President once complained in the National Assembly that a tyre manufacturer had come to him to ask what would happen to his factory if the Tanzam railway was built. There is no doubt that the motor lobby, which is extremely powerful in the United States, put strong pressure on the American government to opt for improving the Great North Road rather than building the rail link.

In the early 1960s aid was seen by many in the West as a panacea for the developing countries. By 1965, however, there was a general disillusionment on the part of Western donors with the impact of aid, and that year witnessed a decline in the flow of financial assistance from the four major Western donors — the United States, France, Britain, and West Germany. Some governments were also reluctant to commit such a large sum to Zambia, and even more so to Tanzania, because of the tense political relations between these two African countries and the West. Aid, Western donors no doubt believed, could be more usefully spent in those Third World countries which were more sympathetic towards Western interests.

One of the major reasons given for Western rejection of the Tanzam project was the enormous cost involved. During the early 1960s it was thought that the line could be built for around £50 million, the 1966 Anglo-Canadian survey suggested a figure of £126 million, and the final Chinese estimate in 1970 was £166 million. These amounts did not include the additional facilities at Dar es Salaam port for handling Zambian cargo, which might have added an extra £10 million to the capital outlay.

The enormous cost of the Tanzam railway caused many Western officials to agree with the World Bank's assessment that 'the urgent need for investments in other parts of Northern Rhodesia and Tanganyika and in other sectors of the economy raises doubts about the advisability of concentrating such a large amount of money on one single project at this time'.[21] It was also believed, with considerable justification, that it is often wiser to invest in a large number of small projects, rather than overconcentrating resources in one area or sector.

The West insisted that the Tanzam railway was a 'political' project and in many senses this was correct. Zambia was determined to break her dependence on Rhodesia because of the dangers of relying on the white South. The Tanzanians and Zambians noted that Western definitions of 'economic' seemed to vary with the occasion. The Anglo-Canadian survey had enthusiastically supported the project, after the World Bank had pronounced it unviable, but even when it was admitted that the line would be economic, no Western offer was made to finance the railway. This suggested that the refusal was based on political rather than economic criteria. Long, turgid economic reports, which kept a number of Western consultant firms in business, appeared to many Tanzanians and Zambians to have been used as a smokescreen for political considerations. The project threatened to become buried under the weight of all the paper that it generated.

The development of Tanzania and Zambian ties with China further antagonized the West and, as Nyerere complained, the British failed to understand the desire of the two African states to compare the advantages of different offers before turning any of them down. Since Britain never offered to finance or build the Tanzam railway, the British attitude was unacceptable to Tanzania and Zambia. The stage was set for China to embark on its largest aid project — a railway from Dar es Salaam to the Copperbelt that was to change the whole geo-political situation in Southern Africa.

# IV

# CHINA'S OFFER

Some scores of years ago, the German colonialists brought to this land over one thousand Chinese workers from Tsingtao, Shanghai and Canton to build railways for them. The hard-working Chinese cut through high mountains and blazed the trail in the wilderness. A group of them lived in a small village at the foot of the Usambara Mountains near Tanga, and they named it 'Shanghai Village'. Some local Tanganyikans still remember that village and recalled that the Chinese had helped their fathers to plant and cultivate tea . . . .[1]

Kao Liang, the senior correspondent of the New China News Agency who wrote these words, was among the swarm of foreign journalists who descended on Dar es Salaam to cover Tanganyika's independence celebrations. His dispatches described how Chinese workers had helped to build the colony's first railway just over 50 years earlier. Kao can hardly have imagined that a decade later 15,000 of his compatriots would be constructing a new line from Dar es Salaam. In 1961, when Tanganyika won its independence, Northern Rhodesia remained under colonial rule and the question of a rail link between Dar es Salaam and the Copperbelt had only just been considered by the African nationalists. The idea of China financing a project of such magnitude would certainly have caused surprised comments in the Tanganyikan and Northern Rhodesian capitals.

Chou En-lai, when he visited Dar es Salaam four years later, came bearing an offer to build and finance the Tanzam railway. Tanzania and Zambia, which had been seeking assistance from the West, were at first reluctant to consider aid from China. But they badly needed the railway, so if Western governments were unwilling to put up the money, then they would have to turn to the East. An initial agreement with China was signed in 1967. Within a few months Chinese surveyors had disembarked at Dar es Salaam and begun laying survey markers along the 1,200 miles to the Zambian Copperbelt.

Western governments, angry that China had succeeded in establishing a 'presence' in territories which had previously been their preserve, warned of the dangers of accepting Chinese assistance and accused Peking of attaching political strings to the railway. For the next few years a constant stream of anti-Chinese rumours were circulated by various sources in an attempt to discredit China's offer. The Tanzanian and Zambian governments, on the other hand, became convinced that Peking's motives in embarking on the project were quite compatible with their own interests. On 12 July 1970, almost a decade after Kaunda and Nyerere had first discussed a rail link between their two countries, representatives of China, Zambia, and Tanzania gathered in Peking to sign the final agreement. The Chinese government had committed itself to its largest aid project in the Third World.

## COOLIES TO ENGINEERS

When Jan Van Riebeeck, who organized the first European settlement in South Africa, arrived at the Cape in 1652 he commented that what was really needed to develop the area was 'some industrious Chinese'.[2] Two and a half centuries later the Dutchman's hopes were realized as 50,000 Chinese workers were 'imported' — an expression still used in South African government publications — to mine Witwatersrand gold.[3] The coloured 'races' provided a vast reserve of manpower to be moved around in order to extract wealth for Europe.

South Africa's use of Chinese labour was to spark off a revealing debate in German East Africa. Should workers be brought in from China to build the country's first railway or would local labour be sufficient? In 1906 the editor of the *Usambara Post* — 'the organ for the spiritual and economic interests of the colonists', as its masthead proclaimed — came down firmly for bringing in the Chinese:

> The Chinese or the native? That is the question that has to be decided. He who chooses the Chinese gives up hope for the native . . . .
>
> The opponents of the Chinese recall the unworthiness of Chinese morality. Frightening horror stories·can be heard . . . . I must concede that the number of crooked Chinese mineworkers in South Africa is astonishing — but are not our own industrial cities in Europe equally beyond hope?
>
> Colonial politics is not the politics of morality, but the politics of

economics. The economic results of the Chinese in South Africa have been exceedingly good. Business circles, company directors, and other European officials in the mines all value the Chinese contribution. They declare that the further emigration of Chinese workers is simply a matter of necessity — and these people must have a better understanding of the situation than the moral theoreticians of the British parliament. Of the 'immorality' of the Chinese we do not have to be afraid — we can deal with that as we do with the natives . . . .[4]

Coolies were imported by the administration in German East Africa from a poverty-stricken China, where the unemployed were numbered in tens of millions, and Chinese labour — as in so many other countries around the world — was used for railway construction. It had been the Chinese, after all, who had helped lay the first railway across the United States, from the Atlantic to the Pacific, during the 1860s, and at that time there was not a single mile of track in China itself. When railways were later built there they were operated by foreign countries — Russia, France, Germany, Britain, and Japan — who had divided the country into 'spheres of influence'.

Now the Chinese returned to East Africa to build another railway. Seventy years after coolies had built Tanganyika's first stretch of track, China was able to provide 15,000 skilled workers, as well as an interest-free loan of £166 million, to construct hundreds of miles of track over difficult terrain. This dramatically shows the extent to which China's technological and financial capacity has developed. The function of the second railway line built by the Chinese in Tanzania differs from that of the first. While the original track had served to open up German East Africa to colonial rule, the new Tanzam — or Uhuru (Freedom) — railway was to increase Zambia's independence by breaking its reliance on white-ruled Rhodesia.

The friendship between China, Tanzania, and Zambia is easier to understand when one considers the transformations that have occurred in all three countries during the twentieth century. The penetration of Tanganyika and Northern Rhodesia by the colonial powers, and their successful struggle for independence, have been compared with China's experience of Western imperialism and her final liberation. A common background of exploitation — and the attempt to escape from oppression — has been an important factor behind the development of Chinese links with Tanzania and Zambia.

In 1965, when the news of a Chinese offer to build the Tanzam railway hit the front pages of the world's press, the relationships of the

two African countries with China were somewhat different. Tanzania
had won its independence almost four years before, but it was only
during 1964 that close ties were established with China. Zambia, on
the other hand, had been independent for less than a year and its
government showed little interest in developing links with Peking.

'When after independence Tanganyika—and later Tanzania
—began to establish contact with your country, we were not really
doing anything new,' Nyerere told Chou En-lai, 'we were merely
resuming a connection which had been broken off.'[5] In 1419 a
Chinese navigator, the eunuch Cheng Ho, had sailed to East Africa,
and as the Chinese pointed out, the trade links that later developed
had been interrupted only because of the impact of European
imperialism on both Africa and China.

At independence Tanganyika recognized Peking and within a few
weeks the Chinese had opened an embassy in Dar es Salaam.
Nyerere, mainly because of his Western education, was at first
suspicious of the communist countries. The People's Republic of
China was, however, too large to ignore and hence the decision to
establish diplomatic relations. This was at a time when the majority of
African states maintained relations with the Nationalists in Taiwan.
Since then China has become an accepted member of the
international community and it is easy to forget the strong pressures
exerted by the United States on Third World governments during the
1960s to withhold recognition from Peking. The People's Republic
appreciated the support provided by Tanganyika during its period of
forced diplomatic isolation.

For the first few years of Tanganyikan independence there were
few contacts with China. The turning-point occurred in 1964. Early
in January it was announced that Chou En-lai, then on his dramatic
ten-nation safari across Africa, would stop at Dar es Salaam, and
Nyerere would reciprocate with a visit to Peking the following month.
A few days later two events in East Africa intervened which led to a
cancellation of both visits—but also soon led to closer ties between
Tanzania and China.

The first was the Zanzibar revolution that toppled the Sultan's
Arab government, only six weeks after the country's independence,
bringing to power a government representing the African majority.
Abdulrahman Babu, the new Zanzibari Foreign Minister, had visited
China in 1960 and for a time he had been employed as a
correspondent for the New China News Agency. China immediately
recognized the new government and offered both development aid

and military assistance. Three months after the revolution, Zanzibar and Tanganyika joined together to form the United Republic of Tanzania. China, unlike the Soviet Union, welcomed the union and managed both to preserve its position in Zanzibar and to extend its links on the Tanganyikan mainland.

The second event that brought Tanganyika and China together, occurring only eight days after the Zanzibar revolution, was the mutiny of Tanganyikan soldiers, protesting for higher pay. After the revolt had been crushed by British troops, summoned reluctantly by President Nyerere, it was decided to reconstruct the Tanzanian armed forces. Requests for foreign military assistance were made to a number of countries. The first offer to be accepted came from China, and Tanzania thus became the only state on the African continent to receive military instructors from Peking. They comprised a mere seven Chinese experts, providing arms training for six months, but a number of Western ambassadors called at State House to give warnings of the dangers of Chinese aid. Nyerere angrily replied that it was only 'a little attempt to be non-aligned'.[6] China, from this small beginning, became an increasingly important source of military assistance to the Tanzanian People's Defence Force and by the 1970s almost all the country's military equipment and foreign instructors were Chinese.

Contacts between Tanzania and China rapidly developed from 1964. In June Vice-President Kawawa and Babu visited Peking, where agreement was reached on £16 million of aid, and four months later a Tanzanian embassy was opened in the Chinese capital. Nyerere himself journeyed to China in February 1965, when a Treaty of Friendship and a trade agreement were signed by the two countries. The visit was reciprocated by Chou En-lai only four months afterwards and in November Kawawa returned to Peking. The brief period of courtship, with its rapid succession of state visits, was soon over. Tanzania had become China's closest friend in Africa.

It was during 1964 that the Chinese first informed the Tanzanian government that they would be willing to consider building the Tanzam railway. The project was probably raised during Kawawa's trip to Peking in June. Ho Ying, the astute ambassador in Dar es Salaam and formerly head of the African section of the Foreign Ministry in Peking, became closely involved in subsequent discussions. Then in February 1965, just before Nyerere left for his first visit to China, a report appeared in the Zambian *Northern News* that the Chinese had made an offer. Since the newspaper was owned by Lonrho, the British company interested in building the Tanzam railway, it was thought that the story might have been published to pressurize the West into assisting with the project.

'I don't care whether I get communist or Western money,' Nyerere snapped to reporters in 1965. 'I want this railway and I'm not going to be stopped.'[7] During Chou En-lai's visit to Dar es Salaam in June, it was agreed that China would survey the Tanzanian section of the proposed railway. When the twelve members of the survey team arrived two months later they were supplied, at their own request, with a dozen tents and several game wardens to protect them from wild animals. The Chinese, however, had little understanding of Tanzanian conditions and they created a somewhat unfavourable impression. Their survey was a meagre eleven pages, little more than a preliminary report, and it was a rather inauspicious start for a project of this magnitude.

At this time Zambia did not have close relations with China. The Chinese survey team was not allowed to examine the Zambian section of the route and, since their report was apparently prepared only in Chinese and Swahili, there was no copy for the Zambians in English. Zambia had recognized Peking at independence and a few weeks later a Chinese embassy had been opened in Lusaka. But at first there was a good deal of suspicion of China among the Zambian elite, so relations between the two countries were strained.

During 1965 a number of incidents, no doubt exaggerated at the time, suggested that China might have been interfering in Zambia's internal affairs. At the beginning of the year a Chinese diplomat had been reported as giving a trade union official a brown paper parcel, in a Lusaka post office, which contained £75 in banknotes. A few months later trouble erupted again over *Revolution,* a magazine which purported to be published in the capital of Albania (China's European ally). An article on 'The Application of Mao's Precepts on Popular Revolution' described Kaunda as 'a capitalist agent' and pointedly remarked that 'the oppression of the people will be avenged'.[8] The Zambian President protested to the Chinese ambassador, who denounced the magazine as a forgery, but the incident soured relations.

Chinese representatives had apparently raised the question of building the Tanzam railway with Kaunda in 1964. Even after the offer was publicized, following Nyerere's discussions with Harold Wilson in June 1965, the Zambians showed little interest in the prospect of assistance from China. Non-alignment was seen by many

Third World governments as a useful means to encourage the great powers to increase their aid commitments to the developing countries. Zambia initially regarded the Chinese offer more as a lever to force a Western bid, rather than a real alternative. The West was certainly worried by the possibility of Chinese involvement—there was a flurry of diplomatic activity, an Anglo-Canadian survey of the railway, and talk of an international consortium—but it soon became clear that Western finance for the project would not be forthcoming.

The turning-point in Sino-Zambian relations occurred in June 1967 with Kaunda's visit to Peking. A £6-million aid agreement was signed, leading to a Chinese commitment to build the 238-mile Lusaka-Kaoma road in the Western Province as well as a radio transmitter for broadcasting to Southern Africa, and Kaunda became attracted to the Chinese model of development. The most important result of Kaunda's trip, however, was the decision to accept Chou En-lai's proposal for assistance with the Tanzam railway. But many Zambians would have preferred Western aid. Even as late as October 1967, just after the initial agreement had been signed in Peking, the Zambian Vice-President announced that the door was still open.

The Chinese offer had been on the table for three years, so why the delay before it was taken up? 'China's attitude changed,' according to the Foreign Minister Vernon Mwaanga. 'After independence we thought that she meddled in our affairs and we didn't want to exchange one master for another.'[9] Probably more important than a development in Chinese policies—since there is little evidence of interference—was a change in Zambian perceptions as old colonially-inherited fears of the Yellow Peril receded.

## CHINA'S AFRICAN COMMITMENT

On 5 September 1967 representatives of China, Tanzania, and Zambia gathered in Peking's Great Hall of the People to sign an agreement which committed the Chinese to building the Tanzam railway. Like subsequent agreements between the three countries, its precise contents have remained a well-kept secret with only the main points publicly known. China formally undertook to finance the project with an interest-free loan and to build, as well as equip, the railway. Actual costs of the line were not yet determined. Estimates suggested a figure of around £100 million, but the amount of China's commitment could not be fixed until survey and design work had been done. This preliminary investigation, to be financed from a Chinese loan, was to be completed within two years. The Tanzanian and Zambian governments reserved the right not to proceed with the project until they had studied the report of the survey and design team.

It is important to consider why the Chinese undertook to build the railway. The Tanzam line is the third largest development project in Africa — after the Aswan and Volta dams — and China's biggest aid commitment. Yet using some criteria Zambia is a richer country than China. Statistics of *per capita* income, admittedly a very crude measure, show that Zambia's figure of £167 is more than twice that of China. 'We are the more appreciative', Nyerere told his hosts during a visit to Peking, 'because we realize that this capital is not surplus to your requirements nor are your technicians otherwise unemployed.'[10] Some forms of Western aid are provided to stimulate industrial production in the donor country. But for China, with an economic system able to employ all its human and material resources, this was certainly not a consideration in building the Tanzam railway.

China's rail system, which carries 80 per cent of the country's freight, is still rather underdeveloped and a study of the Chinese economy concluded that its 'main weakness continues to be the relatively small size of the transport network — in practice, railways'.[11] China now has about 25,000 miles of track, a figure only double that of Britain for a country with an area 40 times the size. The Tanzam railway is longer than any of the existing lines in China.

Yet the Chinese decided to supply 15,000 skilled workers, along with a huge amount of equipment, to build a line in Africa, rather than extend their own rail system. The wisdom of this decision may well have been questioned by some cadres in China. When Nyerere visited Peking in March 1974 the Chinese television showed two films during one evening. The first was of the Tanzanian President's tumultuous welcome and the other on the construction of the Chengtu-Kunming railway in China's south-west. Similarly, the next issue of the *Peking Review* carried extensive reports of Nyerere's trip as well as a feature on the Chengtu-Kunming line. Since this railway had been completed four years before, it seemed that news of the project might have been carefully released to answer internal criticism that resources should be devoted to railway construction in China.

China's entire aid commitments to Africa until 1970 amounted to £350 million and almost half this sum was allocated for the Tanzam railway. Among non-communist countries only Pakistan, presumably because of its strategic importance for China, has received more aid than Tanzania or Zambia. No single Chinese-assisted project has cost anything like as much as the Tanzam railway. Why then did China put such a large proportion of its foreign aid into this one project, rather than spread its assistance more evenly over the Third World?

'As we are poor ourselves, we know how the other poor people feel,' explained the Chinese ambassador in Lusaka.[12] Spoken from the palatial setting of a reception room in the luxurious embassy these words could easily be cynically dismissed as propaganda. There remains, however, a genuine spirit of solidarity with the rest of the Third World, so in this sense China's poverty actually helps to explain its decision to finance the Tanzam railway. 'Our leaders realized that China was rather backward in railway construction,' a senior official told me in Peking, 'but we should help countries which are more backward — this is our internationalist duty.'[13]

The main aspect of Chinese foreign policy since the 1960s has been opposition to the two super-powers. The United States, a capitalist imperialist nation, attempted to isolate China. The Soviet Union, which represents social imperialism (because, claim the Chinese, it is socialist in words, but imperialist in deeds), has been an increasingly dangerous enemy since the development of the Sino-Soviet split in the early 1960s. The Third World offered an important arena for winning friends, and Africa (which had only just broken loose from its European colonial ties) provided China with a new opportunity to escape from isolation. Simultaneously the development of Chinese ties with the new African states would also reduce American and Soviet influence on the continent.

China's offer to consider the Tanzam project was first made in 1964, when the country was making its dramatic entry into Africa. The year began with Chou En-lai's celebrated journey across Africa, taking him to ten nations, and it was on this tour that Chou proclaimed the famous Eight Principles governing Chinese foreign aid. An upsurge in the growth of the Chinese economy made it easier to increase external assistance, so this period witnessed the beginning of substantial aid commitments to Africa. From August 1963 to the end of 1964 agreements were signed with ten African countries for £100 million of assistance (compared with a total of only £25 million that had been committed up to 1963).

The Chinese government believed that the establishment of relations with the newly-independent nations of Africa would help to weaken the Nationalist regime in Taiwan and enable the People's Republic to break out of the isolation imposed by the United States.

Tanzania and Zambia both resisted American pressure to recognize the Nationalist regime in Taiwan. The decision to establish relations with the People's Republic was not taken in the hope of receiving assistance with the railway — Tanganyika recognized Peking at independence, before the project had been seriously considered — but the Chinese government has naturally only been willing to provide aid to those countries which extended recognition. A diplomatic relationship was therefore a necessary prerequisite for receiving aid.

Tanzania and Zambia consistently attacked America's treatment of China as an international outcast, and the two African states fought hard to help the People's Republic to regain her UN seat. This was particularly appreciated during the Cultural Revolution, when China lost a good deal of international support. It was Salim A. Salim, Tanzania's UN representative and former ambassador in Peking, who — much to President Nixon's anger — 'danced' in the aisle of the General Assembly after the historic October 1971 vote that brought China back into the world body. The two African states maintained normal trade links with China and, as the Chinese ambassador in Lusaka pointed out, Zambia had sold copper to Peking since 1969, despite some Western pressure not to sell this 'strategic' commodity. But again the active role that Tanzania and Zambia played in supporting the rights of the People's Republic — bringing China international 'respectability' — was unconnected with the need to secure assistance for the railway.

The year 1964, during which the Chinese expressed their willingness to consider the Tanzam project, represented a turning-point in Tanzanian foreign policy. A series of incidents — alleged American plots, British policy towards Rhodesia, and West Germany's reaction against an East German diplomatic presence in Dar es Salaam — were important factors behind a serious deterioration in relations with the major Western powers. Tanzania's attempt to pursue a more genuinely non-aligned policy, which involved reducing dependence on the West and developing new ties with the East, presented China with a new opportunity in Africa. The independence of Zambia, in the front line in the struggle for the liberation of Southern Africa, also offered the Chinese government an important chance to outflank the United States and the Soviet Union.

In some respects the development of Sino-Tanzanian ties encouraged the United States to take a greater interest in Tanzania. This can be seen as a factor behind Washington's decision to finance improvements to the Great North Road. But the American government prefers to concentrate its resources in those African states which welcome Western investment and take an anti-communist position. The main effect of the growing Chinese 'presence' in Tanzania was therefore to make American policy-makers increasingly hostile towards Nyerere's government. Once the Chinese provided substantial aid to Tanzania, particularly after their offer to finance the Tanzam railway, the Tanzanian government had less need to remain dependent on Western goodwill. China's decision to go ahead with the Tanzam railway could not but reduce the influence of the United States — and the West in general — in Tanzania.

Zambia's relations with the West, mainly orientated towards Britain for historical reasons, deteriorated rapidly during 1965-6 over Wilson's handling of Rhodesian UDI. At this stage Zambia was only beginning to culltivate ties with China. Already, however, comparisons were being made between the attitudes of the two countries. Britain refused to provide Zambia with sufficient financial assistance to impose sanctions against Rhodesia. China, on the other hand, was willing to undertake to finance the Tanzam railway, in order to break Zambian dependence on Rhodesia, before a survey had even revealed the total cost of the project.

'Go home, *bwana*,' said a Zambian Cabinet Minister to a white expatriate, 'we can do without you — all of you. Who's building the great Tanzam railway and our new roads? Not you, *bwana,* but the Chinese.'[14] This remark — quite possibly rather exaggerated (it was quoted by a South African journalist who had previously worked as an assistant hangman) — emphasizes that Chinese assistance symbolized the decline of Western technical superiority, and consequently economic domination, in Africa.

China's involvement in the Tanzam project was also seen as a means of reducing Soviet influence in Tanzania and Zambia. The Soviet Union had been building up its naval strength in the Indian Ocean, including the provision of extensive military assistance to Somalia, and the Russians were also the largest external donor to the liberation movements in Southern Africa. Tanzania and Zambia, in Chinese eyes, therefore represented an area where it was essential that Soviet influence should be minimized.

The two African states never developed close ties with the Soviet Union. Correct diplomatic relations have been maintained, with both Nyerere and Kaunda visiting Moscow in recent years. Soviet loans were offered — £7 million to Tanzania in 1966 and £2 million to Zambia the following year — but difficulties arose in implementing the projects and seven years after the commitment to Tanzania less than £½ million had actually been disbursed. Trade has also remained at a very low level, only 0.1 per cent of Zambia's total trade and 0.5 per cent in the case of Tanzania, so economic links with the Soviet Union are minimal.

Africa, at least since the mid-1960s, has generally been regarded as a relatively low priority in Moscow. Between 1965 and 1968, for example, only £40 million of Soviet aid was committed to the whole of Africa and this sum represented less than a quarter of the cost of the Tanzam project. Since Soviet assistance was not offered on particularly attractive terms, it could be argued that the Tanzanian and Zambian leaders may have felt it was better to avoid potential difficulties in their relations with China by minimizing the Soviet presence in their countries.

Nyerere and Kaunda have always resented the intrusion of the Sino-Soviet dispute into Africa. The Tanzanian leader had first-hand experience of these problems shortly after the Zanzibar revolution in 1964, when Chinese and Soviet attempts to gain the allegiance of leading Zanzibari politicians had a divisive influence on the island's political situation.

During the early 1960s, before close ties were developed with China, Nyerere and Kaunda saw the doctrinal differences between the two socialist giants rather as the King of Buganda had looked upon the Protestants and the Catholics (known as the Inglesa and Fransa, after the nationalities of the missionaries) in the late nineteenth century. The Bugandan King is supposed to have said that if each side claimed that the other brand of Christianity was wrong, then there was no reason why they were not both wrong.

China's ultimate prize in her foray into Africa would have been to win the unqualified support of the Tanzanian and Zambian governments in the Sino-Soviet dispute. Nyerere and Kaunda have been increasingly attracted by the Chinese variety of socialism as a model for internal development. But the two leaders have avoided public reference to Sino-Soviet differences and they have been very careful not to become embroiled in the conflict. China's decision to build the Tanzam railway has presumably, nevertheless, had some effect, even if relatively marginal, in preventing the Soviet Union from establishing closer ties with Tanzania and Zambia.

The Chinese government has seen the Third World as an important Intermediate Zone between the two super-powers. Strengthening the new African nations, to make them more easily able to resist American and Soviet pressures, was therefore seen as an important priority of China's foreign policy. Chinese aid to the Third World has also helped to build up the image of the People's Republic among the developing countries.

The diplomacy of the People's Republic has been compared by some observers with that of traditional China. Imperial China, the Middle Kingdom, demanded tribute from the rest of the world. One study of China and Africa during this period pointed out that 'the rulers of the Celestial Empire considered themselves to be invested with a universal authority' which needed to be emphasized with 'a corresponding act of homage in return'.[15] This was illustrated by a copy of a Chinese painting in the museum in Dar es Salaam which shows the King of Malindi (on the East African coast) presenting a giraffe to an emissary from China in 1431. The People's Republic no longer wishes to exercise sovereignty over the world, in the sense that Imperial China attempted, or become a super-power. China has, nevertheless, become an important source of ideas as well as a powerful spokesman articulating the interests of the Third World.

The Tanzam railway will no doubt strengthen the progressive forces in the Third World. It has reduced Zambia's dependence on the white South, enabling the government to give greater assistance to the struggle for majority rule. The railway should also offer the two African countries an opportunity for development and help to reorientate their economies from the distorted patterns they inherited from the colonial period. China's decision to assist with the Tanzam railway represented a commitment to the forces of change in Africa.

The Chinese refer to the Tanzam railway as a Friendship Route. Their perception of the project can be seen from an anecdote about 'Sino-Tanzanian friendship bananas' recounted by the New China News Agency:

> When the Chinese surveying and designing team was leaving Ifakara, Tanzania, a local peasant representative presented it with two banana trees. He said with deep feelings to the Chinese: 'To mark the friendship of the Tanzanian and Chinese people, I am going to plant these banana trees here, one representing the Tanzanian people and the other the Chinese people. After your departure, these two trees will remind us of the Chinese personnel sent by Chairman Mao and of the days when we lived together in friendship.' When the Chinese engineering and technical personnel returned to Ifakara later, these two banana plants had grown and borne fruit. At the beginning of this year when

President Nyerere inspected the preparatory works for the Tanzania-Zambia railway project in Ifakara, the Chinese personnel offered him some 'Sino-Tanzanian friendship bananas'. President Nyerere ate with pleasure the bananas of friendship.[16]

'The misunderstanding about the friendship between Tanzania and China', commented the Reuters correspondent in Dar es Salaam, arises 'because the benefits to China are intangible, whereas those to Tanzania are tangible, and Westerners find it very difficult to equate the two.'[17]

It is also probably true to say that the Chinese have a rather more long-term view of foreign policy than do many governments. When Nyerere is asked about China's motives he replies with a single word: 'friendship'. This friendship enables China to attain other goals, not always directly connected with Tanzania or Zambia, but part of the Chinese attempt to reduce the strength of its enemies, the two super-powers.

The Chinese Cultural Revolution inevitably had some effect in slowing down negotiations with Tanzania and Zambia. All Chinese ambassadors, with the exception of Huang Hua in Cairo, were recalled to Peking. China was therefore only represented by a *chargé d'affaires* in Dar es Salaam and Lusaka. In August 1967, just three weeks before the arrival of the Tanzanian-Zambian delegation which negotiated the initial agreement on the railway, the Chinese Foreign Ministry had been taken over by a group of 'ultra-leftist' Red Guards. They had criticized Minister Ch'en Yi for pursuing a policy of 'three surrenders and one extinction'—surrendering to American imperialism, Soviet revisionism, domestic reaction, while extinguishing the flames of revolution—and had called for the export of the Cultural Revolution by Chinese diplomats. This faction, which only held power for a couple of weeks, was removed just before the arrival of the Tanzanian-Zambian delegation, but it was symptomatic of the disruptions that were occurring within China.

The Cultural Revolution affected China's relations with Africa in general: the Chinese were preoccupied with domestic issues, temporary economic disruption reduced the country's ability to provide foreign aid, and the activities of Red Guards often gave the country a bad image abroad. At the same time China suffered a number of setbacks in Africa, due to internal political changes within the continent—particularly military *coups* in countries such as the Central African Republic, Dahomey, and Ghana—which were unconnected with Chinese policy.

But friendship with the Third World continued to be an important foundation of Chinese foreign policy. Peking's increasing isolation — due to continued American hostility and growing tensions with the Soviet Union — made it even more important to maintain ties with Africa. China took few initiatives to develop new links with Africa, it is true, but previous commitments were generally honoured. Senior officials in Peking appear to have seen the Tanzam railway as an important priority and Chou En-lai seems to have taken a personal interest in the project. Tanzania continued to maintain excellent relations with China and when Nyerere went to Peking in June 1968 he was the only head of state to visit the People's Republic during the whole year.

By 1970, when the final agreement on the Tanzam railway had been signed, the Cultural Revolution was drawing to a close and China was beginning a new diplomatic 'offensive' in Africa. During 1970 and 1971 eight African states recognized Peking and, following President Nixon's visit to China and her admission to the UN, almost all the remaining countries maintaining relations with Taiwan switched their allegiance to Peking. China has since become a major aid donor to Africa and in 1971-2 £200 million of assistance was committed, compared with a mere £25 million between 1965 and 1968.

## HOSTILE REACTION

'Red Guard Line Chugging into Africa', ran the headline in the *Wall Street Journal*, suggesting that China's 'internationalist duty' was perceived rather differently in the West and in Southern Africa.[18] Editors vied with each other to produce the most horrifying predictions on the Yellow Peril or Red Menace themes. Much of the reporting was simply ridiculous. Nyerere complained to journalists in London that 'even the suits I wear have been adduced as evidence of pernicious Chinese influence'.[19] More serious were rumours circulated within Tanzania and Zambia in an attempt to build up hostility to Chinese assistance. A leading Tanzanian politician, for example, was once forced to urge delegates at TANU's National Conference to dispel reports that the line was being built from bamboo.

Before construction began stories were circulated that the Chinese were incapable of building the railway. The West — partly out of prejudice, but mainly in an attempt to discredit China — had been reluctant to acknowledge the enormous strides that the Chinese have made since liberation in 1949. China, it was claimed, was a backward country without the technology, trained manpower, equipment, and supplies to build nearly 1,200 miles of track across difficult terrain in Africa. With the internal upheavals of the Cultural Revolution, the project would never get off the ground. Some American commentators even went so far as to suggest that China should be encouraged to go ahead with the Tanzam railway just to demonstrate its failure to perform.

The Chinese, however, have successfully doubled their own railway mileage since 1949 and the proficiency of their engineers was amply demonstrated by the successful completion of the Chengtu-Kunming line in 1970. Its route was described as 'a "geological museum" which includes water-eroded caves, underground rivers, faults, drifting sand, gas-filled layers and mud flows'.[20] The line has 653 bridges and 427 tunnels and, out of the 678 miles of track, more than 250 miles consists of bridging and tunnelling. Forty per cent of China's aid to the Third World has been for transport projects and the ability of Chinese engineers has been proved right across the African continent.

Comparisons between the Chinese railway and the American road in Tanzania later demonstrated the ability of Chinese engineers. The Tanzam railway was completed almost two years ahead of schedule, while an American-built section of the Great North Road was finished six months after the specified deadline. Observers compared the building of the two routes with the fabled race between the tortoise and the hare, with the technologically inferior Chinese playing the role of the victorious tortoise. Furthermore, the American road was so poorly constructed that the weight of the heavy Zambian lorries caused it to buckle during the first rains and an extra £2 million had to be allocated to upgrade the highway.

After it became clear that China had the capacity to build the line, and was serious in its offer, critics turned to other arguments and stressed the dangers of accepting help from Peking. Tanzania and Zambia would be swarming with tens of thousands of Chinese workers. While laying the track they would take the opportunity of indulging in subversion and when the line was completed they would remain and settle in Africa.

Subversion was rarely defined, but it clearly covered a multitude of evils. The presence of such a large number of Chinese workers, stretching right across the two African countries, offered a unique opportunity for indoctrination. Kaunda himself had earlier warned that 'China was not bound by the niceties of diplomacy', so her propaganda therefore called for 'special vigilance'.[21] When Chou En-lai visited Dar es Salaam in 1965 the Tanzanian President remarked in a public speech that 'at no time shall we lower our guard against the subversion of our government' and 'neither our principles, our country, nor our own future are for sale'.[22]

During the Cultural Revolution fears of indoctrination by the Chinese in Africa became more credible. Chinese survey workers initially distributed propaganda in 1968-9, until the two African governments informed Peking that this was unwelcome. But handing out copies of Mao's writings — which after all would have been comprehensible only to the more politically sophisticated and literate section of the population — can hardly be equated with subversion. The Tanzanian Transport Minister, when he had been seen with a copy of the Little Red Book, was asked whether this did not make him a Maoist: 'Well I read the Koran and it doesn't make me a Moslem', he replied.[23]

Since the end of the Cultural Revolution, which roughly coincided with the start of actual construction work on the railway, the Chinese have been careful not to distribute propaganda among African railway workers or the peasants along the route. By 1974 what propaganda there was flowed in the opposite direction. Catholic missionaries in Zambia distributed two pamphlets in Chinese — a small red-covered edition of St John's Gospel and the Thoughts of Jesus — leading Peking's ambassador in Lusaka to protest that if the Chinese were not allowed to distribute their Red Book to the Africans he could not see why the Catholics should hand out their publications to the Chinese workers.

When Western and South African sources talked of Chinese subversion they usually hinted that this would involve more than simply distributing copies of Mao's thoughts. During 1964 it had been alleged that China had been attempting to overthrow governments in no less than five of Tanzania's neighbours — Zanzibar, Mozambique, Malawi, the Congo, and Burundi — which created an atmosphere in which talk of subversion appeared more credible. It was never, however, convincingly explained how the Chinese railway workers were going to overthrow Nyerere and Kaunda.

There was even less explanation of why the Chinese should wish to see the downfall of two governments which were particularly friendly towards them. Tanzania has been China's closest African ally for the last decade and internally has opted for a socialist path of

development. In neither Tanzania nor Zambia were there significant
left-wing opposition groups that could have been supported. In any
case, it would have been strange for the Chinese to have 'committed'
£166 million to two governments which they were attempting to
overthrow.

'Why were the Chinese interested in the Tanzam Railway?' asked
the reporter from the London *Daily Express*. 'I think I found the
answer when I was bumping and lurching over Central Africa for the
first time in a light plane. As we passed over the bush and the mighty
rivers and lakes I realized that this vast continent is empty—not only
of white people, but black people too. The Chinese are the only race
in the world with the numbers and capacity for work which could
clear these great empty spaces. If it cost 10 or 15 million lives, what is
that to them if they have a new continent.'[24] In the words of this
nostalgic colonialist, not only would the railway workers spend their
off-duty hours plotting the overthrow of Nyerere and Kaunda, but
they would subsequently refuse to return home when the track was
completed. Thousands, even millions, of Chinese would settle in
Africa.

Old fears of expansion from the densely populated East were
revived. Back in the 1930s a whole book had been devoted to the
Asian threat to South Africa, with a concluding note that 'from the
land of the rising sun, formidable, eager and sinister, the Yellow Man
looks on.'[25] These fears were particularly strong in East Africa
because of the commonly-held belief that the Indian community was
descended from the Asians brought in to help build the railway from
the Kenyan coast to Uganda at the turn of the century. In fact, out of
the 32,000 Indians who came to work on the line less than a quarter
settled in East Africa. But the legend of the origin of East Africa's
Asian community—a group disliked by many Africans because of
their role as traders—lived on. The railways built during the colonial
period had also led to European settlement along the routes. There
was therefore a historical basis linking railway construction with non-
African settlers. It was somewhat ironic that stories of Chinese
settlement in Tanzania and Zambia mainly emanated from Southern
Africa where the governments were actively encouraging immigration
from overseas.

Just two weeks before the official ceremony marking the beginning
of railway construction, a Nairobi newspaper published a picture of a
group of Chinese reading a poster. A caption on the back of the
photograph, which purported to come from the official New China

News Agency, explained that the poster—headed 'The Promised Land'—called for volunteers to work on the railway in Tanzania and those who wished 'to settle in Africa after the said task is complete will receive good land and a house for themselves and their families'.[26] The photograph was obviously a forgery. Since it appeared to have been forwarded by the East Germany-Africa Society it may have been a Soviet-bloc move to discredit the Chinese, although others believed that the CIA was behind this crude attempt to stir up anti-Chinese sentiments in Africa.

Settler stories rose to new flights of fantasy—one Nairobi newspaper reported rumours that ten million Chinese women would be sent to Tanzania to grow rice for China—although it was never explained quite how the Chinese would settle in Africa. Incredible as the reports were, they were clearly an attempt to create anti-Chinese feelings along the route of the Tanzam line. Nyerere, after being questioned by a friend about the dangers of using Chinese railway workers, replied, as he often does, with a question: What happened to the Chinese workers who many years ago had helped to build the Congolese railway? The only trace was the slit eyes of Joseph Kasavubu, Congolese President during the early 1960s, whose grandfather had been a Chinese coolie brought in to construct the Congo's first railway.

Hostile sources also alleged that the Chinese were financing the railway in return for military facilities in Tanzania. These stories had a degree of credibility, since the Tanzanian People's Defence Force had received a great deal of assistance from China, so there was substantial Chinese military equipment in the country. Chinese military aid to Tanzania has topped the £20-million mark and included a naval base at Dar es Salaam (with torpedo and gunboats), an air force base at Ngeregere (with a squadron of a dozen MiG-19 jet fighters), and extensive assistance to the army.

Over the last decade reports have been published that China has been granted port facilities at Dar es Salaam or Zanzibar. A UN report, however, pointed out that China does not deploy naval units in the Indian Ocean and no Chinese warships have ever been sighted in Tanzanian ports.[27] Since it appears that China may need to make a long-distance test of an inter-continental ballistic missile, there has been speculation that telemetry equipment may have been installed in Zanzibar. There was an American satellite-tracking station in Zanzibar during the colonial period, but—despite rumours circulating over the last few years—there is no evidence of Chinese military installations on the island. This is confirmed by an American military report which mentioned that 'it is no breach of security to say that it appears at present that the [missile-tracking] station is a figment of newsmen's imagination'.[28]

With all the different interests opposed to the Tanzam railway — the white regimes of Southern Africa, Western governments, the Soviet bloc, various commercial concerns, and some opposition groups inside Zambia — there was no shortage of anti-Chinese stories and it was often difficult to tell which source was responsible for a particular rumour. Just before the second round of negotiations with China, held at Lusaka in November 1969, a letter was sent to a number of leading Zambians, which purported to come from the British Communist Party (affiliated to Moscow), warning them of the dangers of Chinese aid. Although the letter was almost certainly forged, it was not clear who sent this anti-Chinese warning.

Events were later to prove that the Chinese presence in Tanzania and Zambia — even though huge in numerical terms — had not in fact posed a threat to the two African governments. In Zambia the only Yellow Peril is a small yellow-painted locomotive, nicknamed by the miners, which carries copper ore a few miles from the South Orebody mine to the Rokana refinery. Nyerere, a devout Catholic, was once told that an American newspaper had carried an article in which some bishops warned of the dangers of friendship with China: 'I assume the Holy Ghost is less concerned than the bishops', commented the Tanzanian President, 'otherwise I'd be facing very serious consequences.'[29]

Western and South African warnings about the dangers of Chinese assistance betrayed a belief that the newly independent African states were incapable of looking after their own interests. This attitude — patronizing at best, and often appearing rather more sinister — implied that outsiders knew what was best for Tanzania and Zambia. The leaders of the newly independent states were naturally very angry about the international outcry over Chinese involvement in the railway project. 'We survived 70 years of British rule without becoming capitalists,' Kaunda commented, 'and we can survive five years of Chinese association without becoming communists.'[30]

## POLITICAL STRINGS

Nyerere was at first suspicious of aid from communist countries and, just before independence, in a speech on the Second Scramble for Africa, he claimed that the socialist countries were on the international level 'beginning to use wealth for the purpose of acquiring power and prestige.'[31] Yet by the mid-1960s the Tanzanian President had become convinced that Chinese aid carried fewer strings than assistance provided by other donors.

The two African countries would have been most vulnerable to Chinese pressure during the late 1960s, after the project had been rejected by the West and the Soviet Union, and while negotiations were being conducted with the People's Republic. The Tanzanian and Zambian governments might have considered it wiser to pursue policies which would have won approval in Peking or at least not to take stands which would have positively antagonized the Chinese. There are, however, no clear instances when the two African governments appear to have been influenced in their decision-making by the need to maintain good relations with China. Kaunda was initially reluctant to accept the Chinese offer so he would presumably have been particularly wary of any political strings. Nyerere has been very sensitive to the use of aid as a means of political pressure and on a number of occasions he has rejected Western assistance for these reasons.

Nyerere once commented that he had noticed one rather odd thing about the international reactions to the railway project—the frightening self-revelation of Western attitudes. 'This criticism', he went on, 'implies that in their view aid is always an instrument of domination.'[32] But Tanzania had already experienced a number of instances when Western aid was blatantly employed as a political instrument. West Germany withdrew its military assistance in February 1965, and threatened to reconsider several million pounds of development aid, after East Germany had been permitted to open a consulate in Dar es Salaam. Eleven months later, following an OAU resolution, Tanzania broke off diplomatic relations with Britain over the Rhodesian UDI and the British government responded by freezing a loan of £7½ million. In 1968 this loan, still frozen, was 'withdrawn' after the Tanzanian government announced its refusal to pay the pensions of retired British civil servants who had served in the country before independence. Then three years later, soon after the pensions dispute had been resolved in Tanzania's favour, the loan was again withdrawn after a move to nationalize private housing had affected some British property. Similar pressures have been exerted by the World Bank, which also refused to approve a loan after Tanzania had nationalized private housing.

After the union of Zanzibar and Tanganyika in April 1964 one

Western ambassador told Nyerere:'You'll find that the railroad to Zambia passes through Zanzibar.'[33] This appeared as a scarcely veiled threat that Tanzania would receive Western aid only if the influence of the communist states in Zanzibar was reduced. There were some fears that had Western governments provided assistance for the Tanzam railway, they would try to use this as a lever to put political pressure on Tanzania and Zambia.

By the late 1960s the different attitudes of Western aid donors and the Chinese were being compared. After the withdrawal of West German military assistance in 1965, China provided four patrol boats and trained a marine police unit. During the following year the Chinese gave £3 million of aid to fund some of the projects that were to have been financed by the British loan which was frozen after the break in diplomatic relations following UDI. China had already won the confidence of Tanzania as an ally that could be relied upon for support in an emergency.

Even had the Chinese wanted to exert political pressures on the Tanzanian and Zambian governments by threatening to withdraw their aid, they would probably have found it difficult once the final agreement on the project had been signed in 1970. After construction had begun China could hardly have withdrawn from the project without tremendous loss of prestige in the Third World. If the Chinese government, for whatever reason, had broken its commitment and left the railway only partially completed, then the two African countries would presumably have argued that this ended their obligation to repay the loan.

Will Tanzania and Zambia remain dependent on China now that the line has been built? The Chinese have put a great deal of effort into training local workers so that the two African countries should very quickly be able to operate the line without substantial dependence on Chinese manpower. Railway equipment has a comparatively long life and, although a refusal to supply vital spare parts or additional rolling stock would seriously affect its operation, the equipment could be purchased elsewhere. It is therefore difficult to see how China, even if she wanted to, could exert strong pressure on Tanzania and Zambia now that the railway has been completed.

Soviet assistance with the Aswan dam has not ensured a Russian presence in Egypt, as Moscow discovered when its military advisers were expelled in 1972. China itself, after receiving more than £150 million of Russian aid during the 1950s, later adopted an anti-Soviet position. Governments, if they have sufficient political determination, are often able to resist external pressures from aid donors.

'A railway is a railway; that is what we want, and that is what we are being helped to build', Nyerere commented when work began on the project. 'It will not', he added, 'be a Chinese railway,'[34] There is no evidence that Chinese pressure has led the Tanzanian or Zambian governments to pursue policies, either internally or externally, that they would not otherwise have adopted. The foreign policies of the two African countries have encompassed many stands which coincide with Chinese interests — for example, support for China's membership of the UN, assistance to the liberation struggle in Southern Africa, and criticism of American aggression in Vietnam — but on such issues Tanzania and Zambia would have adopted these positions even in the absence of Chinese aid. All three countries are members of the Third World and they therefore share similar interests over many issues. The basic principles of Tanzanian and Zambian foreign policy were laid down at independence, before ties were established with China, although later contact with the Chinese may have had a very marginal influence on the way certain questions have been viewed in Dar es Salaam and Lusaka.

A crucial distinction must be drawn between influence, which lies in the realm of ideas, and dependence — whether political, economic, or military — which is based on domination. Dependence, in Chinese eyes, is counterproductive since it will ultimately always lead to attempts to assert independence. China's major criticism of the role of the super-powers in the Third World is that they are actively seeking dependents. The Chinese, who during the 1950s experienced a Soviet attempt at economic domination and have since become leading exponents of self-reliance, reject the concept of dependence. To indulge in this discredited tactic would destroy much of China's reputation in the Third World.

'If Mao Tse-tung told all the Chinese to pee at the same time over Africa, we would all be drowned,' one African leader, who had good relations with Peking, once commented.[35] China's size, with a population twice that of the whole of Africa, means that the resulting relationships with Africa seem rather one-sided. The Chinese export goods, capital, technicians, and ideas to Tanzania and Zambia. Traffic in the opposite direction is comparatively small and this is perhaps the inevitable result of the interaction of two nations with 20 million people and a giant with 800 million.

Nyerere was conscious of this difference when he described his country's relationship with China as 'a friendship between most unequal equals'.[36] The Chinese have a relatively long-term view of foreign policy and they have been extremely careful not to indulge in what they call 'great power chauvinism'. The new nations of Africa have been treated as equals and this has scored the Chinese a major propaganda vistory. To attach strings, either political or economic, to the assistance provided for the Tanzam railway would almost certainly have proved counterproductive.

## WORDS INTO ACTION

When China formally undertook to build the Tanzam railway in September 1967 there was almost three years of surveying and negotiating ahead before the final agreement was signed. To lay the organizational basis for the project the two African governments established the Tanzania-Zambia Railway Authority (known as TAZARA) in March 1968. TAZARA was a joint Tanzanian-Zambian public corporation and it was headed by a Zambian Executive Officer with a Tanzanian Deputy. Policy decisions were taken by a Board of Directors (consisting of three Permanent Secretaries from each country), with ultimate power in the hands of an Inter-Ministerial Committee (two Ministers from each country) which met every three months. TAZARA's headquarters were established at Dar es Salaam, with a Zambian regional office at Mpika and a branch office in Lusaka.

The Tanzanian and Zambian Ministers of Transport were the most senior officials responsible for the railway at Cabinet level. Both countries also appointed a Political Co-ordinator with overall responsibility for the project. The Tanzanian appointee, Waziri Juma, was within the TANU bureaucracy, rather than the government, and had served as ambassador in Peking during the early stages of negotiations with China. Timothy Kankasa, the Zambian Co-ordinator, was Minister of State in the Foreign Ministry.

Four major rounds of tripartite negotiations — between China, Tanzania, and Zambia — were held between 1967 and 1970. Amir Jamal, an Asian (Indian) who was Minister of Finance, headed the Tanzanian delegations. The Zambian side was led by Elijah Mudenda, who served as Minister of Foreign Affairs and later headed the Finance Ministry. The second round of negotiations was held in Dar es Salaam shortly after the establishment of TAZARA. On 8 April 1968 the three nations signed two protocols which dealt with financing the preparatory work and the conditions under which

Chinese personnel would serve in Tanzania and Zambia. The most important agreement, however, was a third protocol concerning the survey and design work for the railway.

Just four days after negotiations ended the first party of Chinese surveyors arrived at Dar es Salaam. Preliminary investigations determined the most economical route, taking into account both engineering considerations (including gradients as well as the bridges, tunnels, and embankments required) and economic factors (population patterns and the natural resources of the areas which the line traversed). Planners examined the impact of the railway on the Tanzanian and Zambian economies and estimated the amount of traffic that the route was likely to carry.

Survey teams had to cross remote areas. 'Local villagers flew for their lives as a truckload of Chinese suddenly appeared out of the bush on a survey mission,' one journalist reported, and 'the villagers apparently had never seen a white man, let alone travellers from distant Asia.'[37] Survey work proceeded quickly and small triangular markers began to wind their way to Kapiri Mposhi. When the Chinese surveyors, who numbered around 500, had completed a section, the maps were sent to Peking, where the design work—to determine the plans for the embankments, bridges, and tunnels—was completed. Consideration was also given to the inputs needed for the project: the plant, equipment, materials, locomotives, rolling stock, and buildings.

By the third round of discussions the Chinese team had already finished surveying on the ground and most of the preparatory work had been completed. Kuo Lu, Vice-Minister for Railways, represented China at the Lusaka negotiations, and on 14 November 1969 three documents were signed. A supplementary protocol was approved, concerning the technical principles on which the line would be built, and the minutes of the talks dealt with details of construction work. A supplementary agreement was also approved to extend the line from Kidatu, on the existing East African Railways system, direct to the port of Dar es Salaam. Despite the fact that this involved an extra 200 miles of track, which may have cost an additional £15 million, there were a number of advantages. Since the Zambian gauge ($3\frac{1}{2}$ feet) was larger than that of East Africa (1 metre), the direct link made trans-shipment unnecessary. The line would be under the control of one body, simplifying operations, and under partial Zambian ownership. Finally, the route to Dar es Salaam would open up the agricultural lands south-west of the capital which had been poorly served by transport facilities.

The final agreement was signed at Peking on 12 July 1970. One of the protocols approved the proposals outlined in the 'Report on the Survey and Design for the Tanzania-Zambia Railway' which had been prepared by the Chinese. The financial arrangements—the amount of the loan (£166 million) and the method of repayment—were dealt with in a second protocol. Minutes of the talks laid down the procedure for the actual construction of the railway. The long negotiations were over, the documents signed: Tanzania and Zambia had secured a foreign partner to finance and build their railway.

The Chinese had first expressed interest in the project as far back as 1964. So why the delay before the final agreement? In the mid-1960s this was largely due to hesitation on the part of the two African countries, particularly Zambia, which were rather reluctant to accept Chinese aid and would have preferred Western funds. The UDI emergency, although it had strengthened the determination of the two African states to proceed with the railway, also temporarily diverted the attention of Zambian officials to the country's immediate transport needs.

The very fact that three governments were involved in the project made negotiations more complex. Initially the Zambians did not have the same experience as the Tanzanians in dealing with Chinese officials, and this may have slowed down progress. Step-by-step negotiations enabled the two African countries to observe Peking's performance before they committed themselves further. Internal events within China, particularly the Cultural Revolution, also slowed down decision-making in Peking. Finally the survey and design work—which took a year and a half to complete— had to be finished before the cost of the project was known and the final agreement could be signed.

SOFT TERMS

The Chinese survey of the Tanzam railway estimated that the costs would be 988 million Yuan, equivalent in 1970 (when the final agreement was signed) to £166 million, and an interest-free loan was offered for this amount. This figure included all items—surveying, building, and equipping the railway—but if actual costs were higher, then the additional sum would be provided by China as a grant. A reliable source has in fact claimed that the final price-tag on the project may well exceed £200 million.

The loan was to be available from 1 January 1968, in order to cover surveying costs, and can be drawn on until the end of 1977. After a five-year grace period, until 1982, repayments will be spread equally over 30 years so that the cost of the railway will not be repaid completely until 2012. As the Tanzanians and Zambians have said, it will be their grandsons who will pay for the line. Repayment charges, totalling £5½ million a year, will be met on an equal basis by the Tanzanian and Zambian governments. Originally the possibility had been discussed of Zambia taking responsibility for 60 per cent of the loan, since it will be the major user of the railway, but presumably the Zambian government would then have been entitled to greater control over TAZARA. It was therefore decided that the two African countries should participate equally in the project.

Chinese aid is unique in that it provides for a semi-automatic form of debt reschedulement, by extending the repayment period if the recipient finds it difficult to reimburse the loan. Rescheduling of the Tanzam loan does not appear to have been mentioned publicly. However, a senior Chinese official in Peking told me that it would be favourably considered if a request was made by the Tanzanian and Zambian governments. The Tanzam loan, in accordance with Chinese practice, is interest-free and the absence of interest charges has considerably reduced the cost of the project for the two African nations.

The Chinese loan can be repaid either in third-party currencies or in exports. At present China's major purchases from the two African countries consist mainly of Tanzanian cotton (£5 million in 1973) and Zambian copper (£8 million). If these commodities were used to repay the Tanzam loan they would presumably be accepted at current international prices. Western reports that the Chinese were building the Tanzam railway to gain access to Zambia's copper wealth were therefore incorrect since any imports received as payment for the project would be purchased at prevailing world prices. Increased Chinese copper imports would certainly be welcomed by the Zambian government since greater demand could raise world market prices.

One of the features of the Tanzam project is the high proportion of locally incurred costs—for material, transport, and above all for wages—which in most aid schemes are borne by the recipient. Local costs for the Tanzam railway were estimated at £86 million, or 52 per cent of the total, and it would have been difficult for Tanzania and Zambia to provide these funds from their own resources. China, however, is short of foreign exchange—until 1973 her total trade was actually less than that of Taiwan—so it would have proved a heavy burden for the Chinese to finance local costs in cash.

A commodity credit arrangement was therefore agreed whereby Chinese goods were provided on a credit basis to Tanzania and Zambia, where they were sold through the state trading corporations, with the proceeds used to defray local costs. It was assumed that most of the local costs would be raised through the commodity credit. If, however, the two African countries found it difficult to absorb sufficient quantities of Chinese goods, then China undertook to provide the balance in cash. Tanzania, where 70 per cent of construction costs were incurred, is believed to have obtained £2 million in cash during the first year of the project.

The two African countries have recently absorbed large quantities of Chinese goods, and an ancient trading relationship has thus been revived. More than a thousand years ago China traded with East Africa, mainly through Arab intermediaries, but this ended several centuries ago. At independence neither Tanzania nor Zambia had any trade with China. Since then Tanzanian imports have leapt up to £35 million in 1973 (20 per cent of Tanzania's total) and Zambian imports have reached £6 million (3 per cent of Zambia's total). No tiny village shop in the two countries does not now have at least a few goods from China on its shelves. In Zambian towns, during the early 1970s, one often sat down at the dining table to face a strange mixture of Chinese and South African imported food.

The announcement of the commodity credit arrangement caused an immediate uproar from traditional exporters who feared that the Tanzanian and Zambian markets would be flooded by cheap goods from the East. Britain, Tanzania's most important trading partner during the 1960s, was in fact overtaken by China as the country's largest source of imports in 1971. Kenya, which exported a considerable amount to Tanzania, claimed that the commodity credit was a discriminatory practice, contravening the Treaty of East African Co-operation, that affected the operation of the common market. South Africa and Rhodesia, Zambia's traditional sources of supply, were also hit by competition from China and this was partly responsible for the loosening of Zambian economic ties with the white South.

It was often said that China was providing the commodity credit in order to penetrate the Tanzanian and Zambian markets and, it was pointed out, 47 per cent of China's exports to Africa went to these two states in 1972. Trading patterns, once established, are difficult to reverse as suppliers gear themselves to new lines, learn new servicing techniques, and build up spares, and as consumer tastes develop. On a global scale, however, China's exports to Africa represented less than 6 per cent of her total foreign sales. The Chinese would hardly have provided goods to the value of £86 million — the estimated amount of local costs, which will not be completely repaid till 2012, just in order to open up the Tanzanian and Zambian markets. An American report commented realistically that the terms of the Tanzam loan were 'so soft that if China's principal aim was commercial penetration this would have to be regarded as one of the great 'loss-leader' market entries of all time'.[38]

A Zambian trade mission, returning from Canton in 1969, painted a gloomy picture of trade prospects and reported that a limited range of Chinese goods was available, only a small proportion of these appeared to be good value for money, long delays were likely in shipping, and some products could compete with locally-manufactured goods. These conclusions were unduly pessimistic, and there have been a number of positive spin-offs from the commodity credit, although certain difficulties have developed.

The Tanzanian and Zambian state trading corporations, which handle trade with China, are in their infancy and have faced severe organizational difficulties. Shortages have arisen of certain goods. Large unsold stocks have built up of other products and Tanzania, it was reported, had five million Chinese umbrellas in the warehouses of the State Trading Corporation. Consumers were accustomed to British-style goods, so at first there was some reluctance to switch to new products. Most serious of all, it was feared that imports from China might compete with similar items from local factories or else discourage the establishment of import-substitution plants in Tanzania and Zambia. In the late 1960s, for example, China's major export to the two African states was textiles, and the under-utilization of textile factories in Tanzania and Zambia was partially blamed on this.

Chinese goods — ranging from chewing gum and toy machine guns to bicycles and agricultural equipment — are now widely sold throughout Tanzania and Zambia. Often these products are considerably cheaper than those from traditional sources, although sometimes they are slightly less robust, and most Chinese imports have proved to be excellent value. A change in the trading structure of the two African countries was also a positive step in reducing dependence on colonially-inherited relationships and tapping new competitive sources of supply.

The commodity credit saved Tanzania and Zambia a large amount of foreign exchange during the early 1970s since Chinese goods, almost all of which replaced products previously imported, were obtained on a credit basis. Foreign exchange will not have to be paid out on these imports until the Chinese loan is repaid and this was particularly important for Tanzania when it faced a serious balance of payments crisis in 1974.

Aid from China is tied to Chinese labour, equipment, and goods provided to raise the local costs—yet the terms of the Tanzam loan were very generous. Indeed when the Tanzanian Finance Minister proposed China's membership of the World Bank in 1973, he specifically mentioned that the terms of Chinese assistance were much softer than World Bank loans. It is ironical that had the aid for the railway been provided by the West, which is so much wealthier than China, it would never have been given on such a generous basis.

In 1970, almost a decade after Kaunda and Nyerere had first discussed the possibility of building a rail link between their two countries, work began on China's largest development aid project. Peking called it the Friendship Route, and it was seen as a way to increase the strength of the Third World and weaken the super-powers. In Washington it was regarded as a Red Railway, which would thrust communism into the very heart of Africa, and the minority regimes of Southern Africa saw the line as a threat to their political and economic domination. Tanzania and Zambia christened the project the Great Uhuru Railway because it would strengthen the independence of the two countries. The railway, already heavily charged with political dynamite, was to be built at last.

# V
# BUILDING THE LINE

The Chinese technician blew his whistle and waved a flag as the huge track-laying machine suspended a length of railway line. The steel track with its concrete sleepers was gently lowered: thirty Chinese and African workers leapt forward to prise the line into place while others flicked nuts on to bolts. Then, with a hoot and a roar, the track-laying machine edged forward on to the rails which it had just laid and hoisted another section of track from its back. 'One 12.5-yard length of line every 5 minutes 20 seconds,' explained the Chinese interpreter, 'and there are two 8-hour shifts every 24 hours, so we lay about two miles a day.'[1] After years of requests, negotiations, and surveys, the gleaming steel rails were at last cutting a path from the Indian Ocean to the Copperbelt.

The last decade has witnessed a growing disillusionment with Western and Soviet aid — among both recipients and donors — and an increasing interest in Chinese assistance as an important alternative for the Third World. The theoretical basis on which China provides aid was laid down in the Eight Principles enumerated by Chou En-lai during his visit to Africa in 1964. But little has been published on how these principles have been translated into practice. This chapter examines the techniques which have been used in building the Tanzam railway, to provide a case study of Chinese assistance in action.

## LAYING DOWN THE LINE

'Work first, words later' was the slogan. Construction of the railway began in April 1970 when the results of the survey were available. Three months later representatives of the three countries met in Peking to sign the final agreement on the project and the formal inauguration took place in October. It was reported that Chou En-lai himself might attend the ceremony. In the end, however, Fang Yi, Minister for Economic Relations with Foreign Countries, represented China. On 26 October 1970, just after Zambia had celebrated its sixth anniversary of independence, Kaunda laid a foundation stone at Yombo. Only a few months before it had been a small village on the outskirts of Dar es Salaam, but already it had become a bustling construction depot for the project. Two days later Nyerere officiated at a similar ceremony at the Zambian terminal of Kapiri Mposhi. There, in contrast to the hive of activity at the Yombo site, there was little more than a foundation stone lying next to the track of the existing ZR line.

Speed was essential since the railway was vitally needed to break Zambia's dependence on the white South. It might have been quicker to have begun work simultaneously in both Tanzania and Zambia. Kapiri Mposhi, however, was 1,400 miles by rail from Beira and this was a long haul for heavy machinery and supplies. The real problem was that the existing line passed through Portuguese Mozambique and Rhodesia. These countries would almost certainly have prevented the transit of supplies destined for the construction of a new railway which would divert traffic away from their own routes.

The first length of track was laid at the Kurasini dock, beside Dar es Salaam's sheltered bay, and the route then wound round the southern side of the Tanzanian capital, through groves of coconut palms, to the main construction depot on Pugu Road. One of the first buildings to be completed was the Chinese personnel reception centre, through which nearly 50,000 Chinese workers passed before the track reached the Copperbelt. There was also a hospital, staffed by Chinese doctors, which served those engaged on the project. By early 1971 the equipment depot to handle supplies for the railway was finished and work had also begun on the locomotive and rolling stock repair workshops, a ten-track marshalling yard, and the huge passenger station.

Three routes were used to transport supplies and equipment to the construction sites along the projected railway. The existing EAR line ran to Kidatu, within eleven miles of Msolwa on the Tanzam route, so a temporary track was laid connecting the two rail systems. Extensive use was also made of the Great North Road, and thousands of Chinese trucks — all with the driver's seat on the kerb side — plied the road in convoys. On some stretches as much as three quarters of the traffic was TAZARA transport. Thus the American road helped to build the Chinese railway. Almost all the road signs along the Great North Road were painted in red Chinese characters — an incongruous sight in the African bush — directing drivers to the construction camps. But the most important way of transporting supplies was along the completed section of the railway.

Mobile construction camps, as well as larger base camps, were established along the route. Base Camp Number One, at Mang'ula, was built close to the EAR railhead at Kidatu. The massive workshop at Mang'ula manufactured prefabricated concrete products—sleepers, poles, and slabs—for the line. A sawmill turned local timber into wooden sleepers and other items, such as station furniture, needed for the project. A repair workshop, for both machinery and transport vehicles, was equipped with a foundry (for forging spare parts) and kept the construction equipment in good running order. Chinese trucks—unlike the Fiats of the Zambia-Tanzania Road Services—were never seen abandoned by the side of the Great North Road.

The first stage in constructing the railway was for bulldozers to clear a strip of ground, which had usually been forested or covered with vegetation, and build up the road bed for the track. Altogether 116 million cubic yards of earth had to be shifted before the project was completed. This was equivalent to building a wall one yard high and wide, encircling the globe almost three times.

Mobile camps were established at the site of each of the bridges and tunnels. When the track-laying teams arrived, the bridges and tunnels had already been completed, so work proceeded steadily on laying the line to the Copperbelt. Three hundred bridges, with a total length of nine miles, had to be built and twenty-one tunnels, totalling six miles, were cut. Most of these were located along a fairly short stretch in Tanzania where the railway ascends the Mufindi escarpment.

Sections of track, with concrete sleepers already attached, were assembled at the Mang'ula base camp and transported over the completed railway to the point where they were laid. An ingenious track-laying machine lifted the assembled sections with a crane device, lowered them down on to the completed road bed, and then moved over the new track to lay the next section. Up to three miles of track a day could be completed using this method, with work continuing round the clock. Ballast was put down with another time-saving device which slowly ran along the track, raising the rails several inches with a bar magnet, and automatically evening out the ballast underneath. After the line had been laid it had to be protected against tropical rainstorms by thick grass planted on the sides of the embankments and culverts.

The Tanzam line has a 3½-foot gauge, to match the Zambian railway system rather than the slightly narrower metre gauge of East

African Railways. 'Presumably there is a special site reserved in the British Museum', commented one writer on the Cape-to-Cairo project, 'for the skull of the facetious bureaucrat who, hearing that the British railways heading north from the Cape and south from Egypt were of 3 feet 6 inch gauge, decided that the British railway heading west from Mombasa should be of metre gauge.'[2] The Sudanese line was originally to be built with a metre gauge, hence the decision in the 1890s to use this track in Uganda, but Lord Cromer subsequently decided to alter it to 3½ feet without informing the Foreign Office in London. British officials engaged on the railway from Mombasa to Uganda never heard of this change so they went ahead, followed by the Germans, with the metre gauge. East Africa's track is therefore three inches narrower than the lines to both the north and the south.

When the Tanzam railway was built there were a number of solutions to the problem of incompatible gauges in East and Central Africa. All of them, however, would have increased capital or operating costs. First, cargo could have been trans-shipped from one railway system to the other, either at the East African railhead of Kidatu or at the border between the two countries. Although the use of containers would have reduced the cost of trans-shipment, this would still have raised operating costs. Secondly, the track of the East Africa Central Line could have been converted to the metre gauge. This would have added about £10 million to construction costs. The third solution, which was ultimately adopted, was to build the railway direct to Dar es Salaam.

Since TAZARA and ZR both share the same gauge, rolling stock (both passenger coaches and freight wagons) is interchangeable and can be used on the other's line. Locomotives, however, are normally changed at Kapiri Mposhi where the two systems meet. Goods transferred from the Tanzam line to East African Railways have to be trans-shipped because of incompatible gauges. This can be done either at Kidatu, where a short extension of the Tanzam line meets the EAR system, or at Dar es Salaam.

The Tanzam railway begins at Dar es Salaam — although previous surveys had suggested that the line should start at the EAR railhead of Kidatu — but otherwise the route roughly follows that proposed in earlier studies. Chinese engineers divided the Tanzam line into five sections, each distinguished by geographical and geological factors affecting the engineering problems.

The first section, 312 miles in length, runs south-westwards from

Dar es Salaam up the Ruvu, Great Ruaha, and Kilombero Valleys on the gently rising sides of the flood plains to Mlimba. Almost all the land lies under 1,000 feet and there were few engineering difficulties. Track-laying began at Mang'ula, as well as at Dar es Salaam, and this speeded up completion of the first section. By November 1971 the track had reached Mlimba and to celebrate Tanzania's tenth anniversary of independence the following month three visiting Presidents — Somalia's Barre, Botswana's Seretse Khama, and Burundi's Micombero — were taken by Nyerere for a ride on the railway. The Tanzam project was at last becoming a reality and already it was clear that the line would be completed ahead of schedule.

The second section of the railway, from Mlimba to Makumbako, was described by the Chinese news agency as an area of 'steep mountains, crisscrossing ravines, and primeval forests full of wild beasts'.[3] The line had to rise from the low coastal plain to over 5,000 feet in order to climb the broken Mufindi escarpment on to the Southern Highlands. This part of the route was only 98 miles long, or 8 per cent of the total distance, but it included eighteen of the nineteen major tunnels, many large bridges, and almost a third of the earthworks and rock excavations. It is over parts of this section that the railway reaches its maximum gradient of 2 per cent.

The skills of the Chinese engineers were put to the test: hillsides were sliced away, bridges suspended over ravines, and tunnels threaded through mountains. The longest bridge on the line, over the Ruipa River, is 1,400 feet long and approached by embankments more than 60 feet high at both ends. The Great Ruaha River is crossed by a bridge 990 feet long, supported by 17 pillars (each weighing 350 tons) sunk 60 feet down into the river bed. Another bridge is balanced on pillars 162 feet high. The longest and most difficult tunnel, 2,680 feet in length, leaked large quantities of spring water before it was successfully completed. The track reached Makumbako, atop the Mufindi escarpment, in December 1972 and a magnificent station was built overlooking the vast expanse of the Great Ruaha Valley.

Track-laying continued on the third section of 192 miles from Makumbako, over the Southern Highlands, to the border town of Tunduma. The landscape is mountainous, although not as difficult from an engineering viewpoint as the climb up the escarpment, with the railway reaching its highest point — 5,900 feet — just before the town of Mbeya. The border was just past the half-way point — 602

miles of track had already been laid in Tanzania with another 553
miles to go in Zambia — and it was reached in a little more than three
years after work had begun at Dar es Salaam. The Tanzanian part of
the route, however, was much more difficult, including all the
tunnels and most of the major bridges, and consequently it was
estimated that 70 per cent of the costs would be incurred in Tanzania.

On 27 August 1973 the Tanzanian and Zambian Presidents
journeyed to the border town of Tunduma, where the newly-built
Tanzam railway symbolically passes underneath the frontier control
barrier on the Great North Road, and the two leaders watched the
first section of track being laid in Zambia. Kaunda told the excited
crowd of 20,000 that he hoped to become an engine driver for the
first trip from Kapiri Mposhi to Dar es Salaam.

In Zambia the line crosses gently rolling wooded country at an
altitude of around 5,000 feet. The fourth section of the railway, from
the border to Mpika, included only one major engineering task — the
794-foot bridge across the Chambeshi River — and this section was
completed in June 1974. Work then continued on the final stretch
from Mpika to Kapiri Mposhi, where the last section of track was laid
to join the East African and Central African.rail systems on 7 June
1975. From September the railway was used to haul Zambian goods
as far as the ZR line.

On 23 October 1975 an inaugural ceremony was held at the
terminal of Kapiri Mposhi as the first passenger train arrived from
Dar es Salaam. Kaunda and Kawawa, Tanzanian Vice-President,
were both present for the occasion, along with representatives from
China and Mozambique. Observers noted Nyerere's absence and it
seems that the major ceremony to mark the inauguration of the
Tanzam railway will be held in the middle of 1976 when the project is
finally completed.

'Laying the track up mountains and across rivers doesn't finish a
railway,' commented one of the Chinese workers. 'After come the
problems of getting it operational.'[4] Ballast had to be laid under the
tracks and the earthworks strengthened by planting grass on the
embankments and culverts. Ninety-three stations with sidings had to
be completed, housing provided for the staff, workshops built, and
training schools established. Altogether buildings with a floor area of
3.4 million square feet were constructed. A twelve-channel
communications line was set up along the track and signalling
equipment installed. The railway required seventeen water stations
and eleven electric power plants. Tanzanian and Zambian staff had

to be trained to operate the line.

In 1952 East African Railways had suggested that the rail link should be built over a 21-year period. The Anglo-Canadian survey had estimated that with 'the most advanced earthmoving equipment' the line could be finished within four years, providing construction was begun in Zambia and Tanzania simultaneously, but that 'less extensive mechanisation and more reliance on manual labour would greatly increase the construction period'.[5] The Chinese, using labour-intensive techniques and working only from the Dar es Salaam end, managed to lay the track in less than five years.

'The enemies of our countries are now adopting a new technique to try and discredit the value of the assistance which China is giving us,' Nyerere commented during his visit to Peking in 1974. They 'are now inventing new target dates of their own in the expectation that they will be able to suggest that there has been a delay in completion.'[6] China never specified a completion date, although the target was the end of 1977. But the line was completed in 1975 and all the ancillary works are likely to be finished by the end of 1976.

Early completion is an unusual event in a Third World country with an underdeveloped infrastructure to handle such an enormous project. The co-ordination and planning necessary for such a huge scheme — with a large labour force and vast material inputs — was tremendous. Only three further rounds of tripartite negotiations were held during construction of the railway — in December 1971 (Dar es Salaam), August 1974 (Lusaka), and September 1975 (Peking) — to discuss the building of the line and details were therefore left to TAZARA and the Chinese Railway Working Team. The completion of the project in record time was a tribute to Chinese methods.

DELIVERING THE GOODS

An American 'China-watcher' posted to the Tanzanian capital in the early 1970s apparently spent much of his time staring out of an embassy window, conveniently located overlooking the harbour, to see what was unloaded from the constant stream of Chinese ships. The view was 'impressive, if not depressing', commented one diplomat.[7] As many as 50,000 Chinese workers may have disembarked at Dar es Salaam and over 500,000 tons of equipment and supplies were unloaded.

Trucks, earth-moving machinery, steel rails, bags of cement, locomotives, rolling stock, and other supplies were landed on to the crowded quay in a seemingly endless stream. In just one year, during

1973, 130,000 tons of material were sent from China for the railway
and this amount represented almost one fifth of Tanzania's total
imports by weight. TAZARA was allocated a special berth in the
heavily congested port (already under pressure because it was
handling a substantial part of Zambia's foreign trade), with special
arrangements made for speedy clearance through customs. These
concessions ensured that work on the project was not delayed unduly,
although there were still often several Chinese ships waiting for a
berth. The huge amount of material unloaded also added to the
pressure on the limited handling facilities in the congested port.

A project of this magnitude required a substantial amount of heavy
machinery and equipment. Some was purchased abroad by China
and shipped directly to Dar es Salaam: this included 98 Japanese
Kumatzu bulldozers (worth about £700,000), 1,000 Isuzu trucks from
Japan (valued at £1.3 million), and Scania lorries from Sweden. But
except for some of the earth-moving and transport vehicles, most of
the equipment for the railway was supplied directly from China.

Vast quantities of materials were needed in building the railway.
330,000 tons of cement were used for 3½ million sleepers, tens of
thousands of poles carrying power and communications lines, as well
as for the bridges, tunnels, embankments, culverts, and buildings.
Tanzania and Zambia both have their own cement plants but,
although these supplied part of TAZARA's requirements, they were
unable to meet the sudden demand. Massive quantities had to be
imported from China.

Large amounts of timber were required and initially supplies were
sent from China until TAZARA sawmills were established along the
route. Wooden sleepers were only used on bridges and for some
curved sections of the track. Originally it had been intended to use
them for the Zambian section of the track, because this would have
been cheaper than imported cement, and the timber was to have been
supplied by Zambezi Sawmills. Despite a large investment in the
sawmill to increase its output, supplies remained insufficient. So
cement sleepers were also used in Zambia in order not to slow down
construction.

The Tanzam line has 1,271 miles of track—a basic route of 1,155
miles (single-tracked) and 116 miles of siding—which required
310,000 tons of steel rails. The rails were all imported from China,
mainly from the immense Anshan iron and steel complex in
Manchuria. This proved a heavy drain on Chinese foreign exchange,
since China imports large quantities of steel (£400 million worth in

1973), which is mainly bought from Japan. In order to provide the 1.5 million cubic yards of ballast for the track, as well as the huge amount of crushed stone for making concrete, a string of quarries were opened up along the rail route.

Initially TAZARA were due to operate 102 Chinese locomotives: both 2,000 horse power main-line engines and 1,000 horse power shunting engines. The gleaming turquoise and white locomotives, with Chinese characters for 'The East is Red' emblazoned on the front (after the factory where they are manufactured in China), are already a common sight along the route. The engines are diesel hydraulic-powered, the most economical type for a line with this volume of traffic. China has been manufacturing diesel locomotives since 1956, although a few larger engines are still imported, but her domestic production is limited, so supplying such a large quantity to TAZARA presumably reduced those available for internal use.

Rolling stock has also been supplied by China. 2,100 freight wagons were due to be used to haul Zambia's foreign and internal trade. A passenger service is operating, with both local trains and a Dar es Salaam-Kapiri Mposhi express (doing the journey in under 48 hours), and the Chinese were to supply a hundred coaches. There are three classes: 'Even the Chinese and the Tanzanians want comfort,' commented the TAZARA head, and 'we are not opposed to different classes of coaches.'[8]

One issue that divided Tanzania and Zambia was the question of the braking and coupling system for the railway. Tanzania favoured the use of air brakes (as used on EAR) and Zambia wanted vacuum brakes (as on ZR). The problem apparently went up to Chou En-lai, according to one of the Chinese officials involved in the negotiations, who resolved the 'contradiction'—having made a dialectical analysis of the question—by deciding that the locomotives and rolling stock for the Tanzam line should be equipped with both systems.

It is essential that the locomotives and rolling stock, as well as other equipment needed to operate the line, should be properly maintained. Africa has become a graveyard for Western machinery lying unrepaired because of the shortage of spare parts and technicians. Workshops were established in all the camps while the Tanzam railway was under construction. Two huge permanent workshops have been set up at Dar es Salaam and Mpika, each employing 375 workers, to repair the diesel locomotives and rolling stock, and a smaller workshop at Mbeya will manufacture and repair components. Few spare parts should need to be imported from China and regular yearly servicing should ensure that all the equipment is well maintained.

ZR already had a huge modern workshop at Kabwe and EAR were building a diesel locomotive repair depot at the Tanzanian town of Morogoro. Some observers therefore questioned whether it was economic for TAZARA to establish separate facilities. It is quite possible, on the other hand, that enlarging the ZR and EAR workshops might have cost almost as much as building TAZARA's depots. More importantly, the Chinese always stressed that TAZARA should be a completely self-sufficient line and not dependent on other railway systems.

Every Chinese ship that docked at Dar es Salaam was a reminder of the two African states' dependence on material inputs from the outside world. Originally it had been hoped to make greater use of local materials, such as cement and timber, but unfortunately supplies were often insufficient. Since almost all the imports for the project came from China, along with a few items purchased elsewhere by the Chinese, the stream of ships from the People's Republic emphasized the extent to which aid was tied to goods from the donor.

## USING LABOUR AS CAPITAL

One of the distinguishing features of Chinese aid is the use of labour-intensive techniques. Western-financed projects in the Third World generally use a relatively small number of workers, making extensive use of complex technology and expensive machinery, and this is partly due to the fact that methods used in the industrialized countries are simply transferred. A more important factor, however, is that Western manufacturers are constantly trying to expand their markets and sell equipment to the Third World.

Altogether as many as 100,000 workers — or 1 per cent of the male population of Tanzania and Zambia — took part in the construction of the railway over the five-year period. In 1972 one seventh of Tanzania's paid work force was engaged in the project. Tanzanian and Zambian workers on the project tended to be young, usually in their twenties, and they were recruited on a national basis by radio. Most of the workers originated from the rural areas and inevitably a large proportion came from the areas through which the railway was being built. Only men were employed on the line. Some workers brought their families with them to the construction sites, but often their wives remained at home.

There is a National Service in both countries and it was originally intended to rely on them to provide much of the work force. Tanzanian Vice-President Kawawa at one stage talked of using 30,000 national servicemen, but in the end only a small number actually took part in the project. It had also been hoped that the labour force would be half Tanzanian and half Zambian throughout the project. But this posed a number of problems — wage levels were higher in Zambia than in Tanzania and it proved difficult to find transport and accommodation for foreign workers. So the line was mainly, but not exclusively, built by workers from the country through which it passed.

The work force was divided into teams responsible for different aspects of construction — such as bridge-building, tunnelling, building the road bed, or track-laying — which were in turn split up into a number of sub-teams. A sub-team, forming a camp, would move on to another site after a section had been completed. Workers generally built their own accommodation, usually very small huts with mud walls and grass roofs, which could be put up in a couple of days. The huts, often several hundred of them, would be clustered together next to the Chinese camp and the construction depot. Work on the project was physically demanding and life in the bush was inevitably simple. There was some dissatisfaction over conditions and some workers left TAZARA after a short spell. On the whole, however, industrial relations were excellent — with no strikes — because the attitude of the Chinese, who worked *with* the Africans and did not attempt to boss them around.

The Chinese themselves often use labour-intensive techniques for large-scale construction schemes. It was reported, for example, that 'over a hundred thousand workers and hundreds of thousands of members of the people's militia' had helped to build the 395-mile Hunan-Kweichow railway.[9] China is a developing country — its production of heavy industrial goods is still insufficient for its growing needs — so it 'uses labour as capital' to maximize the human input. Consequently the Chinese would have found it difficult to have supplied the equipment to build the Tanzam railway on a capital-intensive basis.

Labour-intensive techniques were not, however, used for all aspects of construction — track-laying, for example, was done with complex mechanical equipment — but generally the use of labour was maximized. The World Bank estimated that only 1,500 workers would be needed to build the Zambian section of the Tanzam railway. The Chinese, in fact, used almost *fifty times* this number of workers. When construction of the railway was at its height in Tanzania, 50,000 African and 15,000 Chinese workers were employed by TAZARA. A much smaller number of African workers were used on the Zambian section, around 15,000, mainly because the flatter terrain required few major bridges and no tunnelling.

The cost of the project would probably have been higher if capital-intensive techniques had been adopted, and there were a number of positive spin-offs from the intensive use of labour. Labour-intensive methods are often more suitable for a developing country, with a shortage of capital and a surplus of underemployed manpower, so experience in the use of these techniques should help the future development of the two African countries by reducing their dependence on equipment from the industrialized countries.

Labour-intensive methods also helped to create a more egalitarian society in Tanzania and Zambia. On the Tanzam project wage rates for unskilled work were low, about 80 pence a day, but they were comparable to those in other forms of employment. The increase in the size of the wage-earning sector, mainly by the use of previously unskilled workers, helped to avoid a tendency towards the entrenchment of a 'labour aristocracy' — an overpaid élite.

Part of the workers' income was spent near the construction camp, with the remainder often sent back to their families. The injection of this cash into the economy — money which the two governments do not have to repay until after 1983 — was an added stimulus to growth. Demand for foodstuffs increased, because of purchases by railway workers in the camps along the line, and the greater availability of money among the rural population stimulated demand for industrial goods.

'The Uhuru project', commented the Zambian *Daily Mail*, is 'a vast school wherein Zambians and Tanzanians are given an opportunity to acquire valuable and rare skills whilst earning a living.'[10] The most important result of the intensive use of labour was the knowledge, both technical and political, gained by the workers on the project. The Chinese concentrated on demonstrational training, in an on-the-job situation, rather than more formal teaching. Tens of thousands of Tanzanians and Zambians were taught useful skills, such as vehicle maintenance, which should prove to be of enormous benefit to the two countries now that the project has been completed. The use of intermediate technology — for example, using a windlass made entirely out of local materials — helped to take some of the mystery out of machinery and inspire a greater confidence and self-reliance.

Formal training was given to almost a thousand TAZARA workers. Training centres were established at Dar es Salaam and Mbeya while the line was under construction. Each school had between 40 and 80 students, taking two-year courses in subjects such as telecommunications and locomotive driving, for those who would be operating the railway. China also built a permanent training school for 240 students at Mpika which was completed in 1975.

Some of the training schemes ran into difficulties. Two hundred Tanzanian and Zambian secondary school graduates were sent to the North China Communications University, in the suburbs of Peking, for courses in engineering and the financial aspects of railway operation. On their arrival, in June 1972, they were among the first foreign students in China since the Cultural Revolution. Conditions were difficult and they spent their first year learning the Chinese language before beginning their two-year courses. With little entertainment available in austere Peking the students had a rather isolated existence. Their discontent erupted a few months after their arrival, on Christmas Eve, when, following midnight Mass, three Zambians went on the rampage, provoking an incident leading to their expulsion. Early the following year eight other students were recalled by the two African governments.

But despite the personal problems faced by foreign students in Peking, the technical training provided appears to have been well received, and Tanzanians and Zambians should soon be able to fill the senior technical and managerial positions in TAZARA. It is unlikely that more than one or two hundred Chinese experts will be needed to operate the line by 1976 and the number should, it is hoped, be rapidly reduced.

Only 5,600 workers, about 5 per cent of the number who at one time were employed in building the railway, will be needed to operate the line and they will presumably be drawn from among those who participated in construction. A number of other rail projects would, however, be likely to welcome former TAZARA workers. The Chinese have already undertaken to help with the construction of branch lines in south-west Tanzania to exploit coal and iron ore deposits. Consideration has also been given to building a railway from Tabora, on the EAR Central Line, into Burundi as well as continuing the railway on from Arusha to the port of Musoma on Lake Victoria. Zambia has decided to build a link between the Tanzam railway and the Malawian system. Feasibility studies are also being conducted for rail links from Zambia to both Angola and

Mozambique. There is therefore likely to be a demand for railway workers for some years to come.

Most TAZARA workers were formerly peasants and many, having made a certain amount of money, have returned to the rural areas to continue farming. There remains the danger that some, particularly in Zambia, will follow the familiar drift to the towns. Many of the workers will have acquired valuable skills—ranging from driving to bridge-building—which should be useful assets in other fields. The Tanzanian and Zambian governments have a responsibility to ensure that the talents of these men are constructively employed.

### THE CHINESE IN THE BUSH

'The railway will be of tremendous value to my country and free Africa,' Nyerere commented during his visit to Peking in 1974, 'but the example of hard work and selfless service, which is being provided by the Chinese comrades who are acting as technicians and teachers on the railway, may be of equal importance for Tanzania's future development.'[11] The behaviour of the Chinese experts in Africa, in stark contrast to that of their Western and Soviet counterparts, goes a long way to explain the success of China's aid programme in the Third World.

Both Nyerere and Kaunda, and indeed almost all Tanzanians and Zambians who have visited China, have been very impressed with what they saw in the People's Republic. Within the space of a generation China has developed from a feudal and poverty-stricken land into a world power which can provide the basic necessities for all its citizens. For Tanzania and Zambia, which also hope for rapid development and are becoming increasingly frustrated by their inherited models of development, the Chinese example offers great hope.

'It it were possible for me to lift all the ten million Tanzanians and bring them to China to see what you have done since liberation, I would do so,' Nyerere told his Chinese hosts when he first visited Peking.[12] Bringing 15,000 Chinese to Tanzania may have been seen by the Tanzanian President as a more feasible proposition and the opportunity of learning from China's experience has probably been regarded as a useful spin-off from the Tanzam project.

The Chinese model of development has been a source of inspiration in both Tanzania and Zambia. Nyerere and Kaunda frequently refer to the hard work and frugality that they found in China or mention the Chinese emphasis on rural development and self-reliance as important examples for emulation. One can question, of course, how much relevance Chinese practices can have for other societies which have not embarked on the same revolutionary path. But for Tanzania and Zambia, which had previously been brought up with the Western model of development, exposure to Chinese methods of working is likely to have a positive impact on attitudes and policies.

During the mid-1960s, when China's aid to Tanzania began, Nyerere used to jokingly offer foreign journalists £5 for each Chinese they spotted in the streets of Dar es Salaam. The Tanzanian President can no longer afford to make this offer. In 1971 the number of Chinese working on the project had risen to almost 15,000. This figure represented 90 per cent of the total Chinese personnel serving on development aid projects in the whole of the Third World and it was also larger than the number of other expatriates working in Tanzania.

Originally it was believed that considerably fewer Chinese would be required—Nyerere had mentioned a figure of 4,000 in 1969—and the huge number ultimately engaged on the railway was the result of three factors. First of these was the decision to use labour-intensive techniques. Secondly, very few skilled African workers were available for the project. A Tanzanian government publication pointed out that the major obstacle to building the line 'is not so much financial as human—lack of manpower at all levels—planning, administrative, technical and supervisory'.[13] There were only 71 Tanzanian engineers, 23 surveyors, and 2 geologists in the whole country. Finally, the railway had to be completed as soon as possible, since it was to be Zambia's lifeline to the sea. 'I understand that you have the biggest population in the world,' the Zambian Transport Minister told a visiting Chinese delegation in May 1973, 'so that we would like to see one million Chinese railway workers line up from Tunduma to Kapiri Mposhi to complete the railway in two months.[14]

The Chinese sent to Tanzania and Zambia were mainly experienced railway workers and tended to be older than their African colleagues. Many had helped to build the Chengtu-Kunming line, which was officially opened in 1970 only a few days before the final agreement on the Tanzam project. A large number had formerly been members of the People's Liberation Army Railway Corps, a fact which led to Western press reports that the line was being built by military personnel. The Chinese working on the Tanzam project all volunteered to serve in Africa—although the term has a rather different meaning in China where people are generally willing to serve in any area where their skills are needed — and they usually stayed in Africa for a two-year period.

The Chinese workers in Tanzania and Zambia lived a simple and austere life in camps along the route. A number of temporary buildings were constructed, usually made with a timber frame and tar-paper, which served as dormitories. Every Chinese compound had its own vegetable patch, along with a few pigs or chicken, so that they managed to produce 80 per cent of their food. A small sum of pocket money was given to the Chinese workers, with accommodation and food being provided free, and much of the workers' wages — about £15 a month — was retained in China for the workers' families or to await their return.

The Chinese insisted that their aid personnel should not be given special privileges. 'If you die there', Chou En-lai advised, 'do not ask for any special treatment; just have the corpse cremated, and don't let them put up a plaque in your honor.'[15] Ironically Tanzanian and Zambian Ministers attended the funeral of three Chinese workers who had been killed in a road accident, a mark of respect that few Western experts in the two countries have received.

The behaviour of the Chinese was favourably compared with that of Western expatriates serving in Tanzania and Zambia. Westerners in Africa often serve in a directing capacity on a project and take little part in the actual work itself. They have a very high standard of living, usually considerably higher than they would have at home, and their conspicuous consumption tends to have a negative effect on the local society by reinforcing alien values which were imported during the colonial period. The Tanzanians and Zambians — who have seen too many expatriates coming to 'develop' their country from the comfort of an air-conditioned office and a luxurious villa — are certainly very conscious of the different attitude of Chinese technicians.

The dedicated attitude to work of the Chinese made a deep impression on Nyerere and Kaunda during their visits to China. A few years later Nyerere smilingly told a reporter that some Tanzanians engaged on the construction of the railway had come to him to say that if the intention was to make Africans work as hard as the Chinese then they wished he would ask them to leave.[16] The President's comment had been made in jest, for the Chinese never forced their African colleagues to work at their pace, except through the strength of their example. 'When you choose to rest or dodge your duty,' explained one of the Tanzanians on the project, 'these comrades will never bark at you' but 'they will keep on working'.[17]

The Chinese also took part in manual labour—believing that intellectual and physical work should not be separated—which differentiated them from most experts coming from other countries. The Chinese team leader 'wears the same grey overalls and wades in alongside his team', commented the Tanzanian Transport Minister.[18] Some commentators questioned whether it was wise to allow the Chinese to do manual work, thereby depriving African workers of employment, but the positive impact of Chinese participation by far outweighed any loss of employment opportunities.

Kaunda himself, along with a group of Ministers and members of UNIP's Central Committee, spent five days working on the railway during 1974. This exercise, more than a token spurt of physical labour for the cameras, was intended to show his government's commitment to the principle of integrating intellectual and manual work. It was also an attempt to ensure that leaders were not divorced from the people they were supposed to serve. A senior member of UNIP's Central Committee, as he staggered into view balancing two pails of water, commented that 'this exercise gives us a chance to get away from the files and see for ourselves the things which we plan from afar'.[19]

'We are here to work, not to boss around,' the Chinese ambassador in Lusaka commented, 'and this is taught to the workers before they leave China'.[20] The attitude of the Africans—with their bitter memories of colonialism and the behaviour of European expatriates on the Copperbelt—was summed up by a worker when he said that 'had the colonialists worked *with us* in the way the Chinese are doing on the project, Africa would not have been so underdeveloped'.[21] Chinese modesty was shown at Nyerere's farewell banquet in Peking when Chou En-lai asked the Tanzanian government 'to educate our technical personnel working in your country and help them correct their mistakes and overcome their shortcomings'.[22] Few leaders of a great power would adopt such a humble attitude in dealing with a small country like Tanzania.

Despite the very close contact on the work site, there was little social mixing between the Chinese and the Africans. The two groups of workers lived in separate camps, and critical Western and Soviet observers remarked that the social exclusiveness of the Chinese technicians was a sign of arrogance. Even the fact that they tended to be seen in groups was given a sinister connotation. But it should be pointed out that Europeans working in Africa tend to live in certain residential districts and to keep to themselves during their social hours.

There were no female Chinese workers on the Tanzam project, with the exception of a handful of doctors, and the question of female company was much commented upon by the Tanzanians and Zambians. The Chinese, unlike their Western counterparts, never went to the local bars to pick up African girls. President Kaunda himself noted that 'we are yet to see a Chinese coloured ever since they came here', whereas the Europeans often 'leave behind them fatherless coloured children'.[23]

Linguistic problems made social communication difficult — since most of the Chinese did not speak more than a few words of English or the local languages (such as Swahili and Bemba). Interpreters were essential. Chinese officials may have preferred to protect their workers from a partially bourgeois environment. The Tanzanian and Zambian governments were also anxious that Chinese workers should not distribute political propaganda, and social integration might have led to accusations of attempts at politicization. Separation also avoided possible incidents, caused by the mixing of two such different cultures, that could have soured relations between the communities.

The Cultural Revolution sometimes affected the behaviour of Chinese personnel in Africa and a number of 'excesses' occurred in Tanzania and Zambia. This was illustrated by a Sino-American confrontation which took place in southern Tanzania in the early stages of the project. One morning in March 1970 two teams met near the village of Chimala: the Americans, working on the construction of a section of the road to Zambia, and the Chinese who were preparing a survey of the railway. An American bulldozer driver apparently told the Chinese: 'You have come too close to my road, you will spoil it. You must move your line on the other side of the hill.' The Chinese replied, 'Sorry, our preliminary survey shows that we must take this course,' and the small group of workers lay down in the path of the American bulldozer.[24] The unfortunate driver, when he had been forced to stop, was held captive for nine hours until he was rescued by Tanzanian police. Later, when the Cultural Revolution was over, the Chinese would not have intervened so aggressively and they would have almost certainly have informed the Tanzanian authorities, rather than take direct action themselves.

Another example of 'ultra-leftism' can be attributed to the Cultural Revolution. The New China News Agency released a photograph showing a group of a dozen Chinese and African surveyors 'singing revolutionary songs at work-break'.[25] Each worker was holding a copy of the Red Book containing Mao's Thoughts, and the ensemble was led by a Chinese conductor. Later photographs have always avoided such crude propaganda and have been designed to show the two groups of workers labouring side by side, rather than under Chinese leadership.

Since the construction of the railway began in mid-1970, roughly coinciding with the end of the Cultural Revolution, the Chinese have been much more cautious and sensitive towards the wishes of the two African governments. In discussing the project with Chinese officials I have always found that they claim that their assistance was relatively minor — which was of course quite untrue — and that the railway was a Tanzanian and Zambian project. The behaviour of the Chinese technicians in Africa has provided an appropriate example for a developing country. This helped to reduce the negative impact of reliance on foreign experts.

EIGHT PRINCIPLES

The Eight Principles of Chinese aid, printed as an appendix to this book, were first outlined by Chou En-lai during his historic safari across Africa in 1964. They were an attempt to define the differences between assistance provided by Western and Soviet donors, who were under heavy criticism from the Chinese, and the aid offered by China to the Third World.

In general the Eight Principles were consistently applied to the Tanzam project. The Chinese were careful to treat the two African governments as equals and never to infringe their sovereignty. The loan for the railway was on an interest-free basis and only good-quality equipment was supplied. Strong emphasis was put on training, so that local people could take over, and the Chinese technicians in Tanzania and Zambia shared the same standard of living as their African counterparts.

The only one of the Eight Principles which was not applied in the case of the Tanzam railway is the fifth, which calls for 'projects which require less investment while yielding quicker results, so that the recipient governments may increase their income and accumulate capital'.[26] The line was very expensive, with surveying and construction taking many years, and it is unlikely to produce a substantial operating surplus for some time.

'The railway is a special case', a senior Chinese official told me, 'since Tanzania and Zambia considered the line to be of vital importance.'[27] It is interesting to speculate whether the Chinese government would have taken the decision to finance the Tanzam railway today. The line was a traditional 'turn-key' project, with the donor providing almost all the inputs, and the local contribution—except for the huge labour force—relatively small. Much more typical of Chinese assistance to Africa are small-scale projects in agriculture and light industry where methods employed in China, often using intermediate technology, have proved successful.

In some respects the Tanzam railway is the sort of scheme that was criticized during the Cultural Revolution as 'revisionist' because, at least in the short term, it contradicted the principle of self-reliance in some respects. It involved a loan of £166 million (a sum larger than the total annual development budgets of the two African countries), importing most materials and equipment needed to construct the railway, employing 15,000 foreign workers on the project, and building a line whose traffic will consist of Zambia's foreign trade.

The Chinese government itself has decided that acceptance of foreign loans is incompatible with self-reliance; China has had no foreign debts since the early 1960s when its loans to the Soviet Union were repaid. Tanzania and Zambia, however, are not yet in a position to do without foreign aid. Nevertheless the two African governments support the principle of self-reliance. Indeed the concept of self-reliance was an important basis to the Arusha Declaration, approved by TANU in 1967, which has set the path for Tanzania's development.

But the Tanzam railway, at least in the long run, may well increase the self-reliance and independence of the two African states. The project, unlike some development schemes, was not 'sold' by the donor, but the Tanzanian and Zambian governments took the initiative in seeking external assistance. Zambia needed the rail link to break its economic reliance on the white South and thereby increase its political independence. The successful construction of such a complex project, often using relatively simple and labour-intensive techniques, undoubtedly increased the self-confidence of the two African nations. It helped to make modern technology less mysterious and demonstrated that the West did not retain a monopoly of technological knowledge. Actual operation of the railway, it is hoped, should remain in the hands of the Tanzanians and Zambians. Local people have been trained to operate the line, as well as to maintain the locomotives and rolling stock, so that only a relatively small number of Chinese experts will be required to stay on after construction is completed.

Most important of all are the opportunities that the railway opens up for economic development. Exploitation of mineral deposits in south-west Tanzania, which have only become accessible with the completion of the line, will mean that a heavy industrial sector can be created. The railway should therefore lead to structural changes. It is vital to stress, however, that it will not automatically increase the self-reliance of the two African states. All it does is to open up new opportunities.

# VI
# ENGINE OF GROWTH

The Tanzam railway was built to give Zambia a cheap and reliable outlet to the sea. This merely emphasizes the fact that the Zambian economy, perhaps even more than that of most African states, is externally orientated and dependent on economic ties with the industrialized world. Mining, the entire output of which is exported, contributes almost half the country's national income. But this has created an 'island of development', and copper, for the majority of the country's people, often seems to leave little more than gaping holes in the earth. Hence the Zambian government has been anxious to develop other geographical areas and economic sectors.

Tanzania is among the world's poorest countries, with a *per capita* income of under £50 a year, so the Tanzanian government is equally keen to develop its natural resources. Lands suitable for agricultural production and abundant mineral resources in both Tanzania and Zambia have remained undeveloped because it is too costly to transport bulky produce for hundreds of miles over dirt roads. The two governments are therefore hoping that the new railway will promote development along the 1,155 miles of track and open up regions which remained neglected during the colonial period.

The completion of a cheap and reliable transport link between Dar es Salaam and the Copperbelt should also lead to greater trade and economic co-operation between the two African countries. A larger market, which gives greater economies of scale, should encourage industrial growth and reduce dependence on overseas sources of manufactured goods. The Tanzam railway is therefore seen as an important instrument in the struggle against poverty.

The actual construction of the railway had an important impact in stimulating economic activity along the route. Employment was provided to a large number of people in areas where previously there had been few opportunities for paid work. This brought additional cash into the countryside and stimulated demand for agricultural produce. Construction work on the railway also led to the establishment of services—such as piped water, electricity, and medical clinics—which will benefit local inhabitants long after the completion of the project. Many of the plants opened up to produce materials for the railway, such as quarries and sawmills, are still in use now that the line is completed. At Mang'ula, for example, the prefabricated concrete factory, which made rail sleepers, may well be converted to manufacture building materials. Roads built along much of the rail route, giving access to the Great North Road, will provide a useful feeder system to the new railway. Perhaps one of the most important long-term effects of the actual construction will be the impact of Chinese methods of working which was witnessed at first hand by tens of thousands of Tanzanians and Zambians.

TAZARA itself will employ almost 5,600 workers once the railway is fully operational. Almost half the workers will be based in Dar es Salaam and Mpika—with over a hundred at each of the other major stations (Mbeya, Kapiri Mposhi, Mlimba, Chozi, and Kasama)—and the remaining 86 stations in the rural areas will each employ an average of 23 workers. In Tanzania TAZARA is the second largest employer after East African Railways. The permanent impact of the actual construction of the railway, and employment opportunities with TAZARA, will, however, be relatively small compared with the development prospects opened up by the establishment of cheap transport facilities between Dar es Salaam and Kapiri Mposhi.

## PROSPECTS IN ZAMBIA

At independence the Zambian economy suffered from two fundamental distortions: first, an overwhelming dependence on copper exports; and, secondly, underdevelopment in the agricultural and industrial sectors. The lop-sided nature of the economy had had a major impact on the geographical distribution of development. Zambia is a divided nation—cut in two by Cecil Rhodes' railway from Victoria Falls to the Copperbelt—with 'development' over-concentrated in this narrow strip. Forty per cent of the country's population, along with most cash-crop agriculture and industry, is confined to within 25 miles of the line and Zambia has become one of the most urbanized countries in Africa.

Copper gives Zambia the second highest *per capita* income in black Africa (after Gabon). But the lop-sidedness of the economy has concentrated the country's wealth along the old line-of-rail where the urban population, receiving more than 90 per cent of Zambia's gross domestic product, has a *per capita* income of £350. This is more than the national figure of several European states. The remaining 60 per cent of the population in the rural areas, on the other hand, have an average annual income of only £18.

'Zambia in 1964 was a very typical enclave economy,' the Minister of Finance and Development pointed out. 'Except for the small industrial sector along the so-called line-of-rail, the rest of the country was characterized by an absence of the necessary infrastructure to enable economic development to take place.'[1] Transport facilities away from the original line-of-rail were totally inadequate and virtually no tarred roads or railways had been built outside this narrow strip until the 1970s.

The original railway had had a fundamental impact on the development of Northern Rhodesia. Will a new railway from the Copperbelt to Tanzania have a similar effect on the underdeveloped eastern half of the country? Circumstances have changed considerably since the turn of the century when road transport was in its infancy and the railway was the only efficient means of moving heavy goods over long distances. Above all it was the rich mineral deposits, particularly copper, found on the route of the original railway which led to development along the line-of-rail. Extensive prospecting has not shown commercially exploitable mineral deposits along the Zambian section of the Tanzam railway.

Agriculture accounted for only 8 per cent of Zambia's gross domestic product in 1972, with food imports totalling £22 million. Only 4 per cent of the nation's arable land is under cultivation. Kaunda's government, in view of the widening differential between the urban and the rural areas, has declared that the development of the countryside is an urgent priority. It is therefore hoped that completion of the Tanzam railway will stimulate agricultural production in the areas crossed by the line. The most fertile region on the Zambian section of the Tanzam route is around Mkushi, just 50 miles east of Kapiri Mposhi, where maize and Virginia tobacco are grown commercially. This area, however, is already adquately served by transport facilities, since it is close to the original line-of-rail, so the new railway is unlikely to have a substantial impact on production there.

It is in the Northern Province, with an area more than twice the size of the neighbouring country of Malawi, that development has been most hindered by the lack of transport. Much of the Northern Province has a suitable climate for agriculture, with sufficient rainfall and moderate temperatures, but its sandy soils are infertile. A traditional form of shifting cultivation, known as a bush-fellow ash-culture, is practised. Branches are lopped off trees over about ten acres and burnt on a much smaller area of about an acre. The ashes provide a fertile base, lasting for three or four years, and the process is then repeated on another plot of land. Labour-intensive and land-extensive, the bush-fallow method gives low returns and is unsuitable for cash crops. But fertilizers would be difficult to use because of heavy rainfall and leachable soils.

Most farmers in the Northern Province live on subsistence agriculture with cash crops, such as maize and groundnuts, grown in only a few areas. Coffee is cultivated on a small area around Nakonde, with some Virginia tobacco produced near Kasama. During the early 1960s it was hoped that Turkish tobacco could be developed as a major cash crop, with output reaching 1,000 tons by 1970. Actual production was a mere 8 tons, because of falling prices, and within two years Turkish tobacco had been phased out completely.

Beef cattle are raised in the Northern Province, although commercial production is limited, and the railway might well encourage an expansion of ranching on the Chambeshi Plain near Kasama. Zambia consumes more fish than meat. Most commercially-caught fish come from the northern part of the country—particularly the lakes of Tanganyika, Bangweulu, Mweru, and Mweru Marsh—and transport problems have held back the development of the fishing industry. Since, however, the lakes are all at least 100 miles from the nearest point on the Tanzam railway the new route is unlikely to be used for fish marketing.

The railway, by itself, can hardly be expected automatically to increase agricultural production without a whole range of other measures to make full use of the opportunities presented by the new route. Zambia's Second Development Plan, which emphasized the importance of rural development, proposed the establishment of Intensive Development Zones (IDZ) throughout the country. Integrated schemes would provide an improved infra-structure—including transport, water supplies, agricultural ser-vices, and marketing facilities—in underdeveloped areas of good potential.

One of the first IDZs selected—a triangular region between Kasama, Mbala, and Nakonde, close to the Tanzanian border—is traversed by the Tanzam railway. Within this zone a number of local projects were to be set up. One of these is likely to be located at Old Fife, about ten miles from the border station of Nakonde, where there are good prospects for increasing coffee production. Unfortunately the IDZ concept has hardly got off the ground and it is not yet clear whether the projects will go ahead.

In view of the limited agricultural potential of the Northern Province, as well as a lack of serious planning to make use of the opportunities presented by the railway, development is likely to be mainly confined to towns—such as Kapiri Mposhi, Mpika, and Kasama—along the Tanzam route. Kapiri Mposhi was temporarily swelled by railway workers during the period of construction and even now that the line is completed over 300 TAZARA employees are based at the terminal. A glass factory, opened in 1973, has already established an industrial sector in the town. Kapiri Mposhi was little more than a village until the mid-1960s, when its population was just a few hundred, but it has grown dramatically and will be a town of over 10,000 people by the late 1970s.

Mpika, where the Tanzam line diverges from the Great North Road, is the Zambian regional office of TAZARA and the major workshop and training school for the new railway have also been established there. Over a thousand TAZARA workers are based in the town and Mpika's population, which was under 4,000 when construction began, is likely to be four times as large by the end of the 1970s.

Kasama, capital of the Northern Province, was the largest Zambian town on the Tanzam route—with 9,000 people—before construction began. It is almost 600 miles from Lusaka and, until the early 1970s, almost all of this distance was over untarred roads. During the colonial period, when Salisbury was the economic centre of the region, Kasama was still more remote. Completion of the railway has reduced its isolation and a commercial vehicle factory is now under construction there. Originally the plant was to have been located at Kafue, just south of Lusaka, but in accordance with the government's policy of spreading industrial development the Kasama site was selected. In addition to the growth of these three major towns along the Tanzam route, a number of villages—such as Mkushi, Serenje, Chozi, and Nakonde—have already developed into small urban centres.

The Northern Province suffered from a substantial population decline during the 1960s—the fall in population over the route of the projected Tanzam line amounted to between 15 and 30 per cent over a six-year period—because of migration to the Copperbelt and towns along the old line-of-rail. This creates a vicious circle as the most productive members of the population, the younger and more ambitious males, leave the countryside.

The growth of urban centres along the Tanzam route should at least slow down migration out of the province. Demand for agricultural produce will increase and this could well stimulate production in the areas served by the new railway. There remains the danger, however, that even more peasants will be attracted away from the countryside by the proximity of nearby towns, so that agricultural production might actually fall. The Zambian section of the Tanzam route is therefore likely to remain composed of islands of agricultural development, clustered around a few urban centres, and separated by long stretches with sparse population and low production. The Tanzam railway should eliminate, or at least reduce, one of the major obstacles to economic growth in the Northern Province. But the line will not automatically develop the region since a whole range of inputs are essential for development.

OPPORTUNITIES FOR TANZANIA

The Tanzanian section of the new railway passes through areas with excellent economic potential which had previously been neglected because of the lack of transport facilities. Dar es Salaam is the terminal of the line and the city, which has grown considerably since independence, already has a population of over half a million. It is the country's largest port — which also handles substantial traffic for the neighbouring countries of Burundi, Rwanda, Zaire, and Zambia — and its importance will increase with the completion of the Tanzam railway. Indeed this is one of the reasons for the recent decision to transfer the capital to Dodoma, in the underdeveloped centre of Tanzania, in order to spread the benefits of modernization.

When the line leaves Dar es Salaam it passes through a sisal-growing region. The railway then crosses the northern fringe of the Selous Game Reserve, named after a famous German hunter, whose 16,000 square miles make it the largest reserve in the world. It has become the hunting ground of a small number of wealthy foreigners, paying £100 a day to go on safari, but improved transport facilities would make it easier to establish the necessary infrastructure and open up the reserve to more tourists. The main camp at Beho Beho, for example, was only accessible throughout the year by air until the Tanzam railway brought the line within 35 miles of the camp.

The railway then climbs up the Kilombero Valley, known as the 'rice-bowl of Tanzania', which is an area of excellent agricultural potential. As far back as 1909 the German colonial government had considered plans for building a railway through this fertile region and half a century later the UN Food and Agricultural Organization survey emphasized the need for improved transport facilities. By 1964 a branch from the Central Line had been laid to serve the Kilombero Sugar Factory, at Kidatu, which produced almost half of Tanzania's output. Production of other cash crops—particularly maize, rice, cotton, and fruit—is increasing in the Kilombero Valley. Prospects for growing vegetables and raising cattle are also good. The government has stressed the importance of developing this area and a group of Chinese agricultural experts are among those advising on improved methods of farming. In 1966 the Anglo-Canadian survey of the Tanzam project estimated that 200,000 acres of new land could be brought into production with an investment of £60 million. No decision appears to have been taken to embark on such an ambitious programme, mainly because of the enormous capital cost, but the area has an excellent potential.

At Mlimba, previously a small village and already an important station on the railway, the line leaves the Kilombero Valley to climb the heavily wooded Mufindi escarpment, where there are a number of sawmills. The Anglo-Canadian survey suggested the establishment of a massive £30-million pulp factory, near the village of Mufindi, with a yearly output of 250,000 tons. It now seems that a smaller paper plant will be set up and the Swedish government has financed a feasibility study of the project.

The railway reaches the top of the escarpment at Makumbako, already a growing town, and the line then descends slightly into the Usangu Plains before reaching Mbeya. The Usangu Plains are another area of great agricultural potential and a £4-million pilot irrigation project, assisted by the Chinese, has been started on the Mbarali River, ten miles north of the new railway. Eight thousand acres will be irrigated, mainly for growing rice, and other facilities—including a rice mill, a poultry farm, a power station, and a brick factory—are being provided as part of an attempt at integrated rural development.

The Tanzam route then crosses the densely populated Southern Highlands and the two rail spurs, being built to open up iron ore and coal deposits, should also improve the transport facilities in a good agricultural region. The Southern Highlands' fertile volcanic soils, with adequate rainfall, make this an area of similar potential to the rich Kenya Highlands. Tea and coffee are the major cash crops for export. Pyrethrum, a flower used in the production of insecticide, is cultivated and processed at the northern Tanzanian town of Arusha. Maize, wheat, and rice are the main food crops grown in the Southern Highlands. Cattle-raising is also important and three nearby lakes—Tanganyika, Rukwa, and Nyasa—are major sources of fish.

Most of the Tanzanian section of the new railway passes through regions of high agricultural potential. These areas, until the recent improvement of the Great North Road, had been poorly served by transport facilities. Completion of the railway should make it cheaper to send out agricultural products as well as to bring in the necessary inputs, such as fertilizers and machinery. An expansion in agricultural production is also likely to lead to the establishment of processing industries, such as milling and canning, in both the Kilombero Valley and the Southern Highlands.

The extent to which agricultural produce will be transported by the Tanzam railway will depend on the level of tariffs as well as the speed and efficiency of the line. The network of feeder roads will also have to be improved if the main route is to be fully utilized. A substantial proportion of production from the Kilombero Valley (which has poor road links) and the Southern Highlands (distant from the major markets) will probably be railed. In 1966 a total of only 67,000 tons of surplus agricultural produce was grown along the Tanzam route. But the Anglo-Canadian report, perhaps rather optimistically, suggested that with the completion of the railway and an additional investment of £100 million this amount could be increased to 945,000 tons by the end of the century.

The opportunities created by the new railway raised the question of the form that agricultural development should take. Peasants in Tanzania had traditionally lived in isolated settlements. But improved facilities—such as piped water, health clinics, and primary schools—can only be economically provided where populations are concentrated. Back in 1967 the Tanzanian government embarked on a programme to establish *ujamaa* villages (from the Swahili word for 'familyhood'), which group the peasantry in settlements where social services can be introduced. Land in Tanzania belongs to the community, rather than to individuals, and in *ujamaa* villages much of it is farmed communally, with the income divided among the members in proportion to the work performed. It was hoped that this would make it easier to introduce improved farming techniques and increase agricultural production. The *ujamaa* programme represented one of the most ambitious and sustained attempts in a Third World country to improve conditions for the rural population.

Right from the start the government determined that all farming along the Tanzam route should be carried out within *ujamaa* villages. Already about 50 such villages, with an average population of around 400 people, have been set up along the railway, and others are in the process of being established. Kisaki, about 120 miles west of Dar es Salaam, is typical of the new villages to benefit from the opportunities opened up by the line. Rice, maize, and cotton are grown communally by the 160 families of the village, with the surplus marketed through the regional co-operative union. A primary school has been established — in a hut built by the villagers with a teacher provided by the government — and another small building houses a dispensary giving simple medical treatment.

Unfortunately the massive move into *ujamaa* villages during 1973-4 was accompanied by a serious fall in agricultural production, due to a number of factors which included drought, increased fertilizer costs, low government-regulated prices for produce, disruption caused by the movement of large numbers of people, and teething problems within the newly-established villages. The situation became so serious in 1974 that Tanzania was forced to import 400,000 tons of food grains at a cost of £60 million.

The possibility has since been discussed of establishing a huge state farm in a remote area of the Southern Highlands that has been opened up by the railway. The Minister of Agriculture apparently approached the United States embassy to enquire about the possibility of a partnership between an American company, which would put up half the capital, and the Tanzanian National Agricultural and Food Corporation. The projected state farm, growing maize (50,000 acres) and rice (30,000 acres), would go a long way to raise the country's cereal production. Other regions opened up by the Tanzam railway would require a very large capital investment, often for irrigation, and this forced Tanzanian planners to reconsider the role of small *ujamaa* villages.

## MINERAL WEALTH

In the Southern Highlands there is not only fertile soil, but also valuable mineral deposits beneath the ground. The existence of the minerals was known during the colonial period and in 1953 the Colonial Development Corporation had mounted a series of explorations to determine whether they could be economically mined.

This would almost certainly have required a rail link and all surveys of the proposed Tanzam line briefly considered the opening up of this mineral-rich area, but they mainly advised against the 'premature' construction of the railway.

One exception to the generally negative reports was a study prepared by the American Continental-Allied Company in 1963, financed by USAID, that examined Tanganyika's industrial development. It acknowledged that economic discrimination against Tanganyika resulted from the colonial system because East Africa was 'not an area where industrial development received much support' and 'Tanganyika has been at the back of a backwater'.[2] Continental-Allied went on to propose massive investment in the resources of south-west Tanganyika—coal, iron ore, limestone, lumber, and hydro-electric power—in order to develop a whole range of industries. Many products could be manufactured—including steel, coal tar, fertilizers, explosives, and plastics—but some plants would only become economically viable if their output could be sold on the wider markets of East Africa and Zambia.

During the mid-1960s, with the growing determination of the Tanzanian and Zambian governments to proceed with the Tanzam project, the question again arose of developing mineral deposits in the south-west. In November 1967, a few weeks after the initial agreement with China over the Tanzam railway, a group of Chinese geologists arrived to examine some of the areas close to the projected railway, and this was followed by extensive prospecting over the next few years. During Nyerere's third visit to China in March 1974—which included a visit to the Fushun coal mine—the Chinese undertook to assist with the development of Tanzania's mineral wealth. An interest-free loan of £32 million was provided in order to build 155 miles of rail spurs from the Tanzam route to the coal and iron ore deposits. By early 1975 studies of the two deposits had been completed and drilling work to examine the extent of the reserves had already been begun.

Coal deposits in south-west Tanzania exceed 1,500 million tons. A small colliery was established at Ilima in 1953, but this only produces a few thousand tons of coal for local tea estates. The government has now decided to mine the Songwe-Kiwira coalfield, just north of Lake Nyasa, and the Chinese are assisting by building a rail spur to connect with the Tanzam line. Because of the availability of hydro-electric power in southern Tanzania—with schemes under construction or planned at Kiwira and Stieglers Gorge—coal is unlikely to be widely used for generating electricity. Oil and gas can be extracted from coal, a process which could well become economic with the rise in petroleum prices, and this possibility has been discussed with Shell and two American oil companies. Coal also offers an important basis for establishing a chemical industry which could produce coal tar, dyes, pharmaceuticals, and plastics.

The major use for the coal deposits, which are of good coking quality, will be to smelt iron ore and produce steel. Several large iron ore deposits have been found in the south-west of Tanzania and originally attention was mainly focused on Liganga. But, because of the Liganga deposit's high titanium content, the ore would be difficult to smelt and Chinese geologists therefore recommended that the Chunya deposit, to the north of Mbeya, should be utilized. During 1975 engineers from China began work on an engineering study for a rail spur to Chunya.

Processing of iron and steel requires large quantities of limestone and fortunately there are substantial local deposits. Industrial development in this part of the country will also necessitate huge quantities of cement. A £10-million cement factory, being built with Soviet assistance, is under construction near Mbeya and when the plant becomes operational in 1977 annual output should reach 200,000 tons.

The most ambitious scheme is a massive £150-million iron and steel plant, to be established near Mbeya, which will be based on local coal, iron ore, and limestone deposits. It is likely that China will provide much of the financial and technical assistance needed for the project. Initially the plant should produce half a million tons of steel a year and by the early 1980s annual sales could reach the £75-150 million range, providing export markets are available. An iron and steel plant is a vital stage in industrial development since it provides a basis for the establishment of a whole range of ancillary industries.

The new industrial complex will be centred on the town of Mbeya. Before construction began it was the largest urban area on the route of the proposed line, with a population of 12,000, and it is one of the most important stations on the Tanzam route, approximately half way between Dar es Salaam and Kapiri Mposhi. A major TAZARA workshop has also been established there. The heavy industrial complex will increase employment opportunities and rich agricultural lands will be opened up. Mbeya, thanks to the new transport facilities provided by the rail link, will certainly be one of the fastest-growing Tanzanian towns during the late 1970s.

The creation of a metal and chemical industry will have major effects on the Tanzanian economy. First of all it should advance the government's strategy of building up key industries from raw materials through to finished products. This would reduce the need to import products from the industrialized world at increasingly unfavourable terms of trade. Secondly, the need for engineering and machine tool factories, as well as construction material plants, will be increased. Thirdly, there will be a potential for greater linkages between industrial sectors. Textiles, pulp and paper, and metallurgy, for example, are large users of chemicals derived from coal. Finally, a whole new range of potential exports will be produced that could be sold to neighbouring countries. Opening up the mineral resources of south-west Tanzania might well be an important step in changing the whole structure of the country's economy.

In the past development in Tanzania has tended to be concentrated at Dar es Salaam and in certain areas in the northern half of the country. When the Tanzam railway was built no industries had been established along the route, with the exception of the Kidatu sugar refinery, and indeed virtually no industrial development exists anywhere in the southern half of the country. This was partly due to the geographical isolation of the area, with its underdeveloped transport system, and the completion of the railway should therefore have an important impact on the whole pattern of development in Tanzania.

DEVELOPING LINKS

One of the reasons why most African states remain dependent on Europe is that the small size of their internal markets limits the extent of the industrial sector. Co-operation between neighbouring African states offers opportunities to achieve economies of scale, by creating a larger market, and reduce dependence on the industrialized world. Tanzania and Zambia had few economic links during the early 1960s. But Zambia's decision to reorientate its ties away from the white South, along with the development of transport routes to East Africa, has led to a substantial increase in trade.

Zambia's imports from East Africa leapt up from £400,000 in 1964 to £12 million in 1973. Recent figures have been inflated, however, by Zambian imports of refined petroleum from Dar es Salaam. Apart from oil, Tanzania's exports to Zambia totalled £1 million during 1973. Kenyan sales to Zambia, on the other hand, amounted to £7 million, and consisted of a wide range of agricultural and light industrial goods. The fact that Kenya, despite the greater distance, has managed to export so much more is largely accounted for by the greater size of Kenya's industrial sector. Zambian exports to East Africa, divided fairly equally between Tanzania and Kenya, have grown at a much slower rate—rising from £300,000 in 1964 to £1.6 million in 1973—and consist mainly of lead and zinc.

Despite the rapid increase in Zambian-East African trade, impressive in statistical terms because of its level in 1964, the actual amount that is traded is still relatively low and East Africa has only managed to capture a small part of the trade that Zambia has reorientated away from the white South.* There are three major obstacles to the growth of trade, and the first of them is physical.

Overland transport routes between Zambia and East Africa have only recently been developed. During the early 1960s the Great North Road was often impassable during the rainy season, with only eight trucks a week making the slow safari between Dar es Salaam and the Copperbelt, so the usual freight route between the two countries was the 2,500-mile journey by sea from Dar es Salaam to Beira, and then by rail through Mozambique and Rhodesia. Improvements in direct overland transport links between the two countries, particularly the new railway, have therefore gone a long way to reduce the physical barrier.

The second obstacle to the expansion of trade is fiscal. Tanzania is a member of the East African common market, which sets uniform external tariffs, so as long as Zambia is outside this grouping a fiscal barrier remains. Zambia has already applied to join the East African Community, which administers the common market, but a number of fundamental problems remain to be resolved. Because Zambia's tariffs are lower than those of East Africa—although they have been raised substantially over the last few years—increasing them would benefit East Africa by making its exports more competitive, but would result in higher prices for Zambian consumers. Elimination of customs duties on Zambian-East African trade would, however, certainly encourage further development of economic links.

The most serious obstacle to the expansion of trade is structural. The economies of virtually all African states are orientated towards trade with the industrialized world, so that a pattern of dependence has been created in which meaningful development is difficult, if not impossible, to achieve. The East African and Zambian economies are geared to the production of minerals and agricultural produce for export to Europe and North America. As yet, however, there is relatively little demand for these goods in other neighbouring African states.

Zambia faces the further problem of serious trade imbalance with its neighbours, due to distortions created by its dependence on copper. In 1973 East African exports to Zambia were seven times as high as trade in the opposite direction. Zambia offers an attractive market because a relatively high proportion of the population is in paid employment and concentrated in a small geographical area. The country's food production is insufficient for its own needs, mainly because of the large urban population. Thus there are good prospects for East African agricultural exports and the heavy industrial complex in south-west Tanzania might well be able to export part of its output to Zambia. The fact that the Zambian government has reduced its trade with Southern Africa has also created new opportunities for East African exporters.

Prospects for Zambian exports to East Africa are not nearly as favourable. There is little demand for copper, Zambia's major export, while sales of lead and zinc are unlikely to increase substantially. Zambia's agricultural output is insufficient for its own requirements and, because of the infertile nature of the Northern Province, exports to East Africa will probably remain at a very low level. Zambia might be able to increase certain industrial exports, particularly in specialized fields such as mining equipment, but most industries established in Zambia duplicate existing plants in East Africa.

Production costs in Zambia are often greater than in East Africa because of higher wage levels. The average monthly wage in Zambia is £39, compared with £23 in Tanzania. This encourages foreign investors to locate large plants in East Africa. Transport costs, too, although they will be relatively low on the Tanzam railway, are likely to lead to the siting of major industries in East Africa. This would provide cheaper access to seaports for the import of raw materials and, since Zambia's population represents less than 15 per cent of that of East Africa, the major market will normally be in East Africa. Dar es Salaam, benefiting from access to both the Tanzam and East African Railways, should be particularly favourably located for industries serving a regional market.

The trading relationship between Zambia and East Africa has some parallels with the situation that arose within East Africa itself. Kenya became the economic centre of East Africa during the colonial period because the presence of European settlers, its central geographical position, and its relatively developed infrastructure meant that industries tended to be established in Nairobi or Mombasa. Tanzania, as well as Uganda, therefore appeared to be serving as convenient markets for Kenyan exports, but were attracting little development themselves. During the 1960s this caused serious tensions which almost led to a breakdown in East African economic co-operation. So when the East African Community was created in 1967 a transfer tax (similar to customs duty) was instituted to protect infant industries in Tanzania and Uganda.

The pattern which prevailed in East Africa during the colonial period also had parallels within Central Africa. Northern Rhodesia, a member of the Central African Federation, served as a protected market for Southern Rhodesia, while attracting little development outside the Copperbelt. If, now that the Tanzam link is complete, Zambia joins the East African Community, then steps will presumably have to be taken to ensure that a certain proportion of new industries requiring a regional market are established in Zambia.

Tanzania and Zambia have between them the capacity to produce most basic metals and a number of important chemicals. The production of these is likely to lead to the creation of a broad range of industries using metals and chemicals — especially the manufacture of pharmaceuticals, engineering and metal products, pulp and paper, synthetic textile fibres, and explosives — and many of these industries would become more viable if they were serving both the Tanzanian and the Zambian market. The potential for co-ordinated production development is evident, and lower costs would also permit exporting to wider markets.

The danger exists that Tanzania and Zambia may well develop similar industries and thereby lose the benefits of economies of scale. For example, the viability of developing a heavy industrial complex in south-west Tanzania, as the Anglo-Canadian study of the Tanzam railway pointed out, 'would probably have an indifferent chance of success unless it could sell iron, steel, lime, cement, and fertilisers (or at least fertiliser raw materials) to Zambia'.[3] Zambia, however, has already announced that it is establishing its own iron and steel plant at Mwinilunga in the North-Western Province.

Dependence on steel imports would entail certain disadvantages for Zambia: a drain in foreign exchange, reliance on an external source for a vital product, and lost employment opportunities. Co-operation between Tanzania and Zambia would enable some of these problems to be resolved. Zambia could provide part of the capital for the

Tanzanian plant and assume joint ownership. Some Zambian workers could be recruited for the scheme and Zambia, because of its important mining sector, should be able to provide greater technological assistance. Reaching agreement on co-ordinated production development would be difficult. But providing there is sufficient political commitment then these problems could be overcome on an equitable basis.

As long as Africa is divided into fifty-odd separate states the continent will remain vulnerable to economic control from the industrialized world. African unity—at a functional level—appears an essential element in the struggle for economic independence and growth. For Zambia, which has broken most of its ties with Southern Africa, the strengthening of relations with independent African states is particularly important and the Tanzam railway therefore offers a unique opportunity to develop new linkages.

## ZAMBIA AND THE COMMUNITY

'This railway will make Zambia's membership of the East African Community even more natural—and mutually beneficial,' commented Nyerere as he laid the foundation stone to inaugurate the construction of the Tanzam railway, and the development of new ties with East Africa was seen by Zambia as an important element in the attempt to reduce her dependence on the white South.[4] When the East African Community was established in 1967 provision was made for other neighbouring countries to join, and Zambia—along with Burundi, Somalia, and Ethiopia—expressed interest in becoming an associate.

The East African Community has two main responsibilities: it administers the common market and operates a number of shared services. Zambia was particularly keen to join the East African Harbours Corporation, which runs the port of Dar es Salaam, because it was already making extensive use of the Tanzanian port and the outlet would become increasingly important after the completion of the Tanzam railway. Only membership of the Harbours Corporation would give the Zambian government a degree of direct control over such matters as the level of port charges and the expansion of facilities.

Zambia submitted an application for membership of the Community in October 1970. By the beginning of 1971 it was reported that negotiations had reached a fairly advanced stage and agreement between Zambia and East Africa might well have been attained by the end of the year. But the Ugandan *coup*, which brought General Amin to power in January 1971, put an end to hopes of Zambian membership for the foreseeable future. Zambia, like Tanzania, refused to recognize the new regime. Co-operation within the East African Community ground to a halt as Tanzania refused to accept Ugandan representatives in the organization. In June 1971 the Zambian government formally announced the suspension of its request for membership.

Five years after the *coup* serious political differences between Tanzania and Uganda continue to disrupt the Community. Economic difficulties have also developed within the East African corporations, particularly the airways, railways, and harbours, which have incurred massive financial losses. Indeed the numerous difficulties faced by the East African Community have brought its very existence into danger. Until it is on a more effective basis, the Zambian government will hardly be attracted by the prospect of joining the organization. Zambia claims that her application has merely been suspended, to be reintroduced after the political problems caused by the Ugandan *coup* have been resolved. But the prospect of Zambian membership is remote for the immediate future. This is unfortunate since an enlarged Community could lead to a better use of the opportunities presented by the new rail link.

DEVELOPMENT FOR WHOM?

The railways built by the colonial powers in Africa ushered in a period of economic growth which served the interests of the metropole. The economies of the Third World are to a large extent underdeveloped because of the distortion brought about as a result of their integration into the world market from a position of weakness. Their exports and imports are usually determined almost exclusively by the pattern of production and consumption within the rich world, not by their own development needs. Consequently, as the Tanzanian Minister responsible for economic planning pointed out, 'any "development" effort within this distorted pattern is really the *development of underdevelopment*'.[5] Many Third World nations are, in fact, neither 'underdeveloped' nor 'developing', to borrow the usual jargon. They are what Sir Alec Douglas-Home once described in a brilliant slip-of-the-tongue as 'underdeveloping': they are moving backwards.

Political independence brought new opportunities to develop the resources of Africa in a way that would benefit the inhabitants, rather than enriching outside interests, and this was an important factor behind the decision to proceed with the Tanzam rail link. The Great Uhuru Railway, it was hoped, could become an escape route from neo-colonial control. But traffic on the line, at least in the immediate future, will consist largely of Zambia's overseas trade—copper exports and imports of manufactured goods—although the Tanzam railway could ultimately prove an important step towards the development of the two African countries which it serves.

The completion of the Tanzam railway has created a 'development corridor' running 1,155 miles from Dar es Salaam to Kapiri Mposhi. If we consider that the impact of the line may extend up to 25 miles on both sides of the track—and with the present lack of supporting network these are likely to be the limits—then the railway could potentially affect an area of nearly 60,000 square miles or about 9 per cent of the area of the two African countries. Just over a third of the railway's route runs parallel to the Great North Road, but for much of the way the line passes through areas which are poorly served by transport facilities. At present there is no significant industrial development along this route and, with the exceptions of Mbeya and Kasama, no towns had a population of over 2,500 when work began on the project. This gives an idea of the relatively underdeveloped nature of the region which the railway traverses.

The World Bank study of the Tanzam project pointed out that the low level of development in the areas served by the new line would not justify the expense of a railway. But this argument can be reversed: rich agricultural land and proven mineral deposits could not be exploited because of inadequate transport facilities. Development depends on communications, and a rail link, providing there is a good system of feeder roads, is certainly important for opening up remote areas of the two countries.

'Are we really preparing for the Tanzania-Zambia Railway agricul-turally?' one Zambian Member of Parliament asked, 'or are we just waiting for the railway to come here to import things from other people to make Zambia a dumping ground?'[6] The railway, by itself, is unlikely to promote extensive development along the route and, in addition to improved communications, a whole range of inputs is essential. A regional market, encompassing Zambia and East Africa, could support a much greater range of industries than any of the countries could hope to win on a purely national basis. But again this is only made more feasible, not inevitable, by the new rail link. It is not yet clear to what extent the Tanzanian and Zambian governments are going to take advantage of the opportunities offered by the Tanzam railway.

The railway by itself will not automatically lead to a form of development that will benefit the masses — it is merely an instrument in the hands of the governments and people of two countries — but it has opened up important new opportunities that could well have a catalytic effect on the economies of Tanzania and Zambia. The line helps to create the material infrastructure for the long path to economic independence and self-reliance.

# VII

# LIBERATION STRUGGLE

The Uhuru—or Freedom—railway was seen as an important element in the liberation struggle to free Southern Africa from minority rule. Zambia, lying in the front line in the fight for justice, shared 1,600 miles of frontiers with white-ruled territories until the independence of Mozambique and Angola. Its geographical position gives the country a unique strategic importance in the liberation struggle. But at the same time Zambia's dependence on the white regimes of Southern Africa, particularly reliance on its traditional transport route through Rhodesia and Mozambique, endangered the country's independence. As Nyerere remarked, during a visit to Zambia, 'the freedom of a man with an enemy's rope around his neck is not very great'.[1]

Kaunda was initially attracted by the Gandhian concept of non-violence and Zambia has always attempted, whenever possible, to encourage peaceful change in Southern Africa. But by the 1960s it had become clear that the minority regimes were unwilling to surrender power and the failure of sanctions against Rhodesia also emphasized the weakness of relying on non-violent means. Guerrilla warfare, and hence a protracted struggle, came to be seen as an essential element in the process of freeing the white South.

Tanzania and Zambia have undoubtedly been the two members of the OAU who have done most to assist the liberation struggle, and the two governments have closely co-ordinated their policies towards Southern Africa. Nyerere and Kaunda meet frequently for discussions and the white South is always high on their agenda. Their position was summarized most cogently in the Lusaka Declaration, jointly drafted by them in 1969, which called for a peaceful transfer of power to the black communities. If the white regimes in Southern Africa refused to accept this principle, the statement continued, then armed struggle was inevitable.

Zambian dependence on transport routes through Rhodesia and Mozambique became increasingly dangerous with the successes of the liberation movements. On 9 January 1973, following allegations that the Zambian government was allowing guerrilla fighters to operate from its territory, Rhodesia closed its border between the two countries. Freight trains carrying Zambia's foreign trade no longer crossed the beautiful span over the Zambezi. Kaunda—in the knowledge that the Tanzam outlet would be completed within a couple of years—decided that this was the moment to make a decisive break with the white South.

## UHURU LINE

The decision to proceed with the Tanzam railway in the early 1960s was based on an acknowledgement that the Zambezi River was, at least for a time, the great divide between black and white Africa. Decolonization in Southern Africa, despite the 'winds of change' which were sweeping down the continent, was likely to be considerably slower because of the presence of powerful European settler communities. Zambia's dependence on transport routes through the white South—governed by the very regimes which Kaunda wished to see overthrown—made the country extremely vulnerable to external pressures. A reliable rail outlet through black Africa was essential to preserve Zambia's newly-won independence and to enable the government to assist the liberation movements.

As we have seen, Zambia, along with Tanzania, has contributed more to the liberation struggle than any other member of the OAU. The liberation movements maintain transit camps in Zambia and, most important of all, guerrilla fighters are allowed access to the territories still under white rule. South Africa has always recognized the strategic importance of bordering states like Zambia and has tried to create a fringe of 'buffer states' along her frontier with black Africa. 'The really valuable conquest', commented the South African Foreign Minister in 1968, 'and the one which would consolidate the [Southern African] bloc and make it impregnable would be Zambia.'[2] But the Zambian government, re-orientating its links northwards, refused to become integrated into a Southern Africa dominated from Pretoria.

'The greatest single threat to Africa', explained John Vorster, 'is that the Communist Chinese have established a bridgehead in Tanzania, and the possibility that they might, through the construction of the Tanzam railway, infiltrate farther into the heart of Africa and establish themselves on a permanent basis.'[3] Both government officials and the press in the white South painted a frightening picture of Chinese-trained terrorists boarding a train at

Dar es Salaam to disembark at Victoria Falls—armed with Mao's Thoughts and Kalishnikov rifles—ready for combat.

The minority regimes, particularly Rhodesia and South Africa, also opposed the Tanzam project on economic grounds. During the colonial period Northern Rhodesia had become an economic appendage of Southern Rhodesia—which in turn was dependent on South Africa—and Zambia was a lucrative market for the white South. Zambia's reorientation of its economic links northwards to black Africa, including the decision to build the Tanzam railway, hit the pockets of businessmen in Southern Africa.

The minority regimes were therefore anxious to prevent the establishment of transport links to Dar es Salaam. Already a number of communications installations have been sabotaged, presumably by agents of the white South. At the end of 1969 a pumping station on the Tanzania-Zambia oil pipeline was blown up and this temporarily disrupted Zambia's supply of this essential fuel. The following year the road to Dar es Salaam was cut for a short time when a major bridge across the Great Ruaha River was destroyed. Over the last few years a number of attempts have also been made to sabotage the main ZR line between Victoria Falls and the Copperbelt.

A railway, because of its length, is a particularly difficult target to guard against sabotage. Indeed the word 'sabotage', derived from the French *sabots* (meaning the clamps holding the steel rails on to the sleepers), was first used in connection with attempts to derail trains in France before World War I. The Tanzam railway, in view of its vital political and economic significance, would no doubt be a particularly attractive target for the white South. The need to protect communications links to Dar es Salaam, particularly the new railway, has necessitated co-ordination between the Zambian and Tanzanian governments over sensitive issues of security. Special TAZARA police units, numbering almost a thousand men, were formed in both Tanzania and Zambia. The Tanzanian People's Militia, which has been established in all the *ujamaa* villages along the route, has also been responsible for guarding the railway. All bridges, tunnels, and other installations along the Tanzam route are permanently guarded. Security is very tight and even senior civil servants involved with the economic implications of the Tanzam railway have found it difficult to gain access to the route without thorough documentation.

The minority regimes are unlikely to launch a full-scale military attack against Zambia or Tanzania—because of the international outcry that it would produce—but they could well have attempted to disrupt the construction or operation of the Tanzam railway with isolated sabotage attempts. In January 1974, for example, the Tanzanian *Daily News* reported that saboteurs, who had recently struck four times, had tried to derail a train. Many other incidents presumably went unpublicized.

By 1974 the danger of sabotage to the railway was receding: after the *coup* in Portugal the possibility of Portuguese agents disrupting the line gradually disappeared; at the same time South Africa, because of its attempt to improve relations with Zambia and the rest of black Africa, would have been unlikely to attack the railway openly; and Rhodesia, which is becoming increasingly isolated in Southern Africa, might also be reluctant to antagonize the Zambian government. There remains the danger of 'unofficial' attempts by extremist groups to disrupt traffic on the route. Former South African defence head General Melville, for example, revealed a plan for South African volunteers to enter Zambia and Tanzania in order to 'launch reciprocal terrorist attacks, sabotage installations, bridges, railways and particularly the Chinese built Tanzania-Zambia railway'.[4]

When construction began Nyerere stressed that the railway must be guarded 'against the effects of hostile propaganda, for the governments of the south could achieve their objective by political subversion and by spreading disunity as well as by placing high explosives on the line'.[5] Over the last decade a constant stream of hostile rumours, many with an anti-Chinese flavour, have been circulated in an attempt to discredit the project.

Opposition to the Tanzam railway has always existed in certain areas of Zambia. The decision to reorientate economic links northwards to East Africa inevitably affected the Southern Province, which straddled the rail and road route northwards from Victoria Falls to Kafue. The African National Congress, the main Zambian opposition party until the establishment of a one-party state in 1973, always had its main base of support in the Southern Province. The Congress—both as a cause and as a result—adopted a more conciliatory attitude towards the white South, while criticizing UNIP's decision to confront the minority regime by forging new transport links to Tanzanian ports. The Tonga-speaking people of the Southern Province gave less support to the UNIP government, even after the ANC was disbanded, and in the December 1973 elections Kaunda only polled 42 per cent of the votes there (compared with 88 per cent in the country as a whole). Kaunda's decision to build a rail link to Dar es Salaam was only one of the reasons for dissatisfaction in the Southern Province. But it was certainly dangerous to alienate support in an area where the minority regimes could exploit internal political divisions by encouraging opposition groups. The white South did all it could, both from outside Zambia and within, to prevent the construction of a rail outlet through Tanzania.

BLOCKADE

The Tanzam railway's greatest impact on the liberation struggle was made before the line had been built. Kaunda, in the knowledge that the link would be completed within a few years, was able to resist Smith's attempt to blockade Zambia. On 9 January 1973 the Rhodesian government announced that its border with Zambia would be closed for security reasons. The previous day a landmine had blown up a patrol vehicle near Victoria Falls, killing two members of South Africa's para-military forces, and a guerrilla attack had been launched on a village just a hundred miles from Salisbury.

The Rhodesian authorities said that the border posts would remain closed until 'satisfactory assurances' were obtained from the Zambian government that they would no longer 'permit terrorists to operate against Rhodesia from their territory'. Zambia had ignored previous warnings, such as the threat made by the Rhodesian Secretary for Transport, just two months earlier, to cut the country's rail and road links if the Zambian government continued to support 'terrorist activity'.[6] 'I know the Bantu pretty well', Smith confided to a South African reporter soon after the border closure, 'and I believe that this is the sort of thing that they understand.'[7]

The 450-mile frontier between Rhodesia and Zambia, running for its entire length along the Zambezi River, was closed. The two road bridges, at Chirundu and Kariba, were shut. Barriers were lowered over the Victoria Falls Bridge and the white line across the middle of the delicate structure became a new flashpoint. The bridge of Cecil Rhodes, originally intended to link Southern and Eastern Africa, now firmly separated the two regions.

Within a few hours of the Rhodesian announcement came further news from Salisbury that copper exports would be exempted from the ban. Half of Zambia's copper production was then being railed southwards over the Victoria Falls Bridge, providing RR with a lucrative source of traffic, and Smith presumably realized belatedly the financial costs involved in refusing Zambian freight. Another reason for the Rhodesian *volte-face* was that the rebel leader, who had apparently closed the border without consulting the Portuguese and South African governments, was taken aback by the reactions of his neighbours. Mozambique's economy, which remained dependent on transit traffic, was seriously hit by the loss of Zambia's foreign trade. South Africa was attempting at this time to develop links with black African states to the north of the Zambezi and Smith's closure of the Rhodesian border complicated this process. Both Lisbon and Pretoria made it clear that they were angry about the unilateral Rhodesian move.

Less than four weeks after Smith closed his border with Zambia, it was announced in Salisbury that the frontier would be re-opened on 4 February as 'the objectives in closing the border with Zambia have been achieved'.[8] Kaunda flatly denied that he had given any assurances about withdrawing support from the liberation movements and the Zambian government has continued, as before, to provide Rhodesian guerrilla fighters with transit facilities.

'I am afraid we are no longer prepared to put our eggs in Smith's basket', Kaunda commented after the border closure, because 'there they will break.'[9] The Zambian government bravely determined to end its dependence on the white South once and for all. The country would have to develop alternative transport routes for its foreign trade and this decision was only possible in the knowledge that the Tanzam railway would be completed shortly. At the time of the border closure the track had reached Makumbako and six months later the first section of track was laid in Zambian territory.

In the meantime emergency measures had to be taken to keep Zambia's trade flowing. In 1972, the year before the blockade, half the country's foreign commerce was sent through Rhodesia. Zambia, by closing its southern border, was making a greater sacrifice than any other UN member to implement sanctions against the rebel regime. Soon after the border closure the UN Security Council met to consider Zambia's plight and decided to send a mission to Lusaka to examine the situation on the spot.

Zambia faced an enormous logistic problem. The country's imports are more than double the weight of its exports, because of refined copper's relatively high value-to-weight ratio, so the major problem was how to bring in the country's two million tons of imports. By 1972 a number of alternative routes had been developed to reduce Zambia's dependence on Rhodesia. Oil, accounting for 26 per cent of the country's imports, was transported by pipeline from Dar es Salaam. Twelve per cent of Zambia's imports were brought in by truck from Tanzania and eight per cent on the Benguela railway from Angola. The UN mission recommended that general imports should be allocated to Dar es Salaam (504,000 tons), Lobito (272,000 tons), Mombasa (264,000 tons), and Nacala (204,000 tons), with the remainder (180,000 tons) airfreighted into Zambia.

Nyerere, in a gesture of solidarity, announced that Tanzania was willing to divert most of its traffic to the northern port of Tanga (and to a lesser extent to Mtwara) in order to provide capacity for Zambia — as well as Burundi, Rwanda, and Zaire — at Dar es Salaam. This offer represented a major sacrifice by Tanzania since it would have added to transport costs — both financially and by creating bottlenecks — but the UN mission considered that such drastic action was impractical. Dar es Salaam, they concluded, could handle up to two million tons of cargo annually if various measures were taken, for instance if clearance from the port was speeded up.

The UN mission overestimated the capacity of Dar es Salaam and in 1973 the port only handled 196,000 tons of Zambian imports (up by 70 per cent from the previous year), which was much less than the amount foreseen by the UN. Half Zambia's imports were brought in via Lobito (416,000 tons), with smaller quantities shipped through Nacala (100,000 tons) and Mombasa (98,000 tons), and from Southern Africa (34,000 tons). The overall level of general imports in 1973 — 844,000 tons — was down by a third from the previous year, because of tougher import licencing (introduced just before the blockade) as well as transport problems associated with the blockade. During 1974 imports rose to 963,000 tons and similar proportions were shipped through the same ports.

The Tanzam railway had already reached Makumbako and an impressive station had been built just 50 yards from the Great North Road. Immediately after the border closure the Tanzanian Transport Minister announced that a daily train would carry Zambian cargo to Makumbako, where it would be transferred to trucks for the long road haul to the Copperbelt. A few days later, however, this decision was reversed and it was not until April 1974, when construction was further advanced, that the line was used for Zambian traffic. TAZARA then operated up to three trains a month carrying cargo to the village of Mwenzo, a former Christian mission just inside the Zambian border, and from March 1975 the railway was used to bring Zambia's imports as far as Mpika. Then in September 1975, when the track had been completed to the Kapiri Mposhi terminal, the new line was used to haul Zambian imports all the way to Lusaka and the Copperbelt. Within a year 40,000 tons of imports had been carried across the border. More extensive use of the route, according to TAZARA officials, would have interfered with the transport of construction materials, slowing down the project, and congestion at Dar es Salaam port would have made it difficult to handle more of Zambia's foreign trade.

The border closure had a number of harmful effects on the Zambian economy. Copper production was reduced by about 15,000 tons in 1973 because of problems associated with the blockade, although this was partly compensated for by a rise in price caused by lower output. Exports to Rhodesia and South Africa, amounting to £7 million in 1972, fell to only £1 million. Tourism dropped by about a third because fewer visitors entered the country from the south. Shortages of certain imports, particularly materials used in other industries, caused problems. It was also feared that temporary shortages of consumer goods in Zambia might spark off discontent against the government's decision on the blockade. In general, however, the difficulties caused by the border closure did not turn out to be as serious as many people had expected.

The cost of developing alternative emergency routes during the three-year period until the end of 1975 was estimated by the UN mission at £110 million and Zambia hoped to recoup most of this sum in the form of foreign aid. By mid-1974, however, the amount pledged by other countries had reached only £24 million and it seems that the Zambian government will have to bear.much of the cost. Zambia Railways has lost about £5 million a year since the border closure. Little traffic is hauled along the 300 miles from Victoria Falls to the Copperbelt, since most cargo is either railed the much shorter distance to the Zaire frontier or else transported by road to Tanzania. Costs of exporting copper have, interestingly enough, actually fallen by about £1 a ton since the border closure because of relatively low rates on road traffic to Dar es Salaam and Mombasa, as well as a rebate on the Zaire section of the railway to Lobito which is allowed when shipments exceed 150,000 tons a year. Import costs, on the other hand, rose by 55 per cent in 1973 and much of this increase was due to diversion from the RR route.

The decision to reduce economic ties with Southern Africa, despite its short-term cost, benefited the Zambian economy in the long run. New domestic energy sources were opened up and a substantial number of import-substitution factories have been established to manufacture goods previously imported from the south. In 1965 Zambia imported 67 items from Rhodesia, each with a value of more than £100,000, and by 1976 only five of these products will have to be purchased abroad. 'The blockade is a blessing in disguise,' Kaunda commented a few days after Smith closed the border. 'It gives us a golden opportunity to correct Zambia's false start.'[10]

In Kaunda's words, Ian Smith was 'the foolish man who proverbially started cutting the branch on which he was sitting'.[11] The minority regimes suffered four major losses as a result of the blockade. First, Rhodesia and Mozambique lost Zambia's lucrative transit trade. Copper exports had effectively subsidized RR's other traffic and the railway's £15-million deficit in 1974 was largely a result of losing Zambian cargo. RR had been paid in hard currency, so this also involved a loss of foreign exchange and therefore tightened sanctions against the rebel regime.

Mozambique is particularly dependent on transit traffic, which provides 35 per cent of the country's national income, and was thus also affected by Rhodesia's decision to close her border with Zambia. Mozambique Railways lost substantial traffic on the lines to Beira and Lourenço Marques. The two ports in Mozambique were also hit by the diversion of Zambian goods, although to some extent these losses were made up for by increased traffic on the routes to Nacala (via Malawi) and Lobito. The loss of transit revenue was mainly responsible for Portugal's anger at the Rhodesian decision to close the border.

Secondly, the closing of the frontier made it considerably more expensive to ship goods to Zambia from Rhodesia and South Africa — although some trade was conducted via Botswana — and this reduced Zambian imports from the white South. Imports from Rhodesia fell from £7 million in 1972 to £4 million the following year, and almost the whole of this amount was paid for electricity from the jointly-owned Kariba plant, so that the rebel regime lost valuable foreign exchange. South Africa had been Zambia's second most important source of imports, after Britain, and sales dropped from £35 million to £25 million after the blockade. Kaunda's government was in any case trying to reduce trade with South Africa. But this process was certainly accelerated by the border closure. The outlook became bleak for businessmen in Southern Africa who had envisaged Zambia as a gateway for the economic penetration of black Africa.

Thirdly, the rail route through Rhodesia and Mozambique to the port of Beira became an open target for attack by guerrilla fighters in Mozambique, since it was no longer used for Zambian traffic. FRELIMO attacked the Beira-Umtali railway on New Year's Eve in 1973, derailing a train, and during the first half of the following year there were almost a dozen major attacks on the line. The closing of the railway also hit Rhodesia because Beira is the nearest port to Salisbury and 20 per cent of Rhodesia's trade was sent via this route. FRELIMO had begun to enforce sanctions against the rebel regime in Rhodesia.

Finally, the blockade polarized the situation in Southern Africa by reducing many of the remaining linkages between the minority regimes and the independent nations north of the Zambezi. It affected South Africa's hopes of a 'dialogue' with black Africa and strengthened the resolve of the OAU to opt for a confrontation in the liberation struggle. Rhodesia also lost what had been one of the strongest weapons in its armoury: the threat to blockade Zambia. The weapon had been used; it had failed because by the time it was applied Zambia had gained sufficient strength to resist and it could never be used again.

Since mid-1972 there has been a dramatic increase in guerrilla fighting inside Rhodesia and the border closure was a desperate measure to deal with Smith's internal difficulties. The rebel leader no doubt felt that he had to find an external enemy to strengthen white support. Zambia was the only available scapegoat and what could be more dramatic than the public humiliation of President Kaunda? But Smith made a serious error in misjudging Zambia's ability to use alternative routes. It was even reported that he was unaware that the Great North Road had already been tarred for its entire length to Dar es Salaam. Rhodesia had waited too long and the Zambian government — in the knowledge that the Tanzam outlet would soon be available — decided to end its dependence on the white South once and for all. Future historians may well date the beginning of the fall of minority rule in Rhodesia from the fateful day when Smith lowered the barrier across the Victoria Falls Bridge.

THE WEAKENING LAAGER

The growing strength of the liberation movements in the Portuguese colonies, particularly in Mozambique and Guinea-Bissau, was largely responsible for the *coup* of 25 April 1974 which freed Portugal from half a century of fascist rule and ended Europe's oldest colonial empire in Africa. FRELIMO had already liberated about a quarter

of Mozambique—much of the two northern provinces of Cabo
Delgado and Niassa, a good part of Tete, and some of Manica-
Sofala—with a population of about one million. Following the *coup*
in Lisbon the Portuguese government agreed to withdraw from its
African colonies and on 25 September 1974, exactly a decade after
the armed struggle had begun, FRELIMO participated in the
transitional government. Mozambique won full independence on 25
June 1975.

After the closure of the Rhodesian border, Zambia had begun to
use the excellent port of Nacala, in northern Mozambique, as an
emergency outlet. Freight was sent from Lusaka over the Great East
Road into Malawi and at Salima cargo was transferred by rail to
Nacala. After the political changes in Mozambique, which made this
route politically acceptable, increasing quantities of Zambia's foreign
trade were routed through Nacala.

The Malawian railway is being extended from Salima, through the
capital of Lilongwe, to the Zambian border. This £12-million section
is being financed by the South African Industrial Development
Corporation and an initial survey of the project by a South African
company was completed in June 1975. Over the last decade Malawi
has been pressing Zambia to agree to a rail link between the two
countries, which would provide Zambia with an alternative outlet to
ports in Mozambique. But as long as Mozambique remained under
colonial rule, Zambia was unwilling to proceed with the project.

In May 1974, during Kaunda's first visit to Malawi for over a
decade, it was decided to start building the link between the Tanzam
line, near Serenje, and the Malawian border. The railway to Malawi
will provide Zambia with an additional outlet to the sea, as well as
improving communications in Zambia's Eastern Province and
encouraging trade with both Malawi and Mozambique. It has not yet
been announced who will finance the Zambian section of the
line—although Lonrho and the World Bank, who both refused to
build the Tanzam railway, have been mentioned—and the project is
likely to cost over £25 million. The rail link to Malawi will not be
completed until the 1980s, so that it will not compete with the
Tanzam line for some time to come. Discussions have also been held
on the construction of a direct railway from Mozambique through the
Zambezi Valley into Zambia. But this project is in a still more
preliminary stage and is unlikely to be built for many years.

The prospect of independence for Mozambique altered the whole
strategic situation in Southern Africa and seriously weakened Smith's

position in Rhodesia. Three-quarters of Rhodesia's trade with the outside world was sent via ports in Mozambique. But a FRELIMO government in Lourenço Marques could well decide to close its harbours to Rhodesian trade once independence was won.* Botswana would then presumably refuse to allow the Rhodesians to transfer all their trade to the long meandering railway which goes from South Africa, through Botswana, to Bulawayo.

Rhodesia shares a short border with South Africa and since the 1920s the possibility had been discussed of building a direct rail link between the Rhodesian railhead in Rutenga and the South African border at Beitbridge on the Limpopo River. UDI, which increased Rhodesia's dependence on South Africa, made the rail link more important and work finally began on the line in May 1972. Construction was speeded up after the Portuguese *coup* and the link completed in September 1974. But the new railway only has the capacity to carry a small part of Rhodesia's foreign trade, rail charges will be higher than on the traditional route to Mozambique, and South Africa's eastern ports were seriously congested during the mid-1970s. For a decade Zambia had suffered from problems in railing its foreign trade, because of Rhodesian actions, and now the situation looked as if it would be reversed: Zambia suddenly had a number of reliable rail routes available, while Rhodesia's lines were being cut off.

With the prospect of independence for Mozambique and Angola, South Africa saw the necessity for adapting to the new situation. It was essential to learn to live with black neighbours and hence the need for 'detente'. Support for Rhodesia was becoming an increasingly embarrassing burden, so Pretoria decided to put pressure on the Smith regime to reach a settlement with the black nationalists.

Zambia, too, wanted a settlement of the Rhodesian problem. The border closure had been a serious blow to the Zambian economy, at least in the short term, and a re-opening of the Victoria Falls Bridge would have eased Zambia's transport problems. This factor became even more important in August 1975 when the Benguela railway was cut after clashes between the Angolan liberation movements. Consequently both South Africa and Zambia wanted a rapid solution to the Rhodesian problem.

The detente exercise began late in 1974 when the leaders of the Rhodesian liberation movements, who had been locked up since before UDI, were suddenly released. Joshua Nkomo, of the

*Mozambique closed its border with Rhodesia on 3 March 1976.

Zimbabwe African People's Union (ZAPU), and Ndabaningi Sithole, of the Zimbabwe African National Union (ZANU), were permitted to fly to Lusaka for talks. There they agreed to unite under the banner of the African National Council (ANC).

Smith was in a dangerously exposed position; he was forced to negotiate with the very men that he had branded as 'terrorists'. Some leading members of the African National Council in exile would have been in danger of being imprisoned if they returned to Rhodesia. Consequently the ANC refused to consider constitutional talks inside Rhodesia. Smith, for his part, was unwilling to participate in negotiations outside Rhodesia and hence an unusual compromise was reached.

The confrontation between the rebel regime and the ANC was held in August 1975 on the Victoria Falls Bridge. A luxury railway coach — the inappropriately named White Train — was supplied by South African Railways for the occasion. There, 350 feet above the swirling waters of the Zambezi, the two sides faced each other. But the gulf between the black and white leaders was too great and, as widely predicted, the talks quickly broke down.

Soon afterwards the ANC split into factions, the former ZAPU and ZANU groups. The ZAPU faction continued to hold talks with the Smith regime, but the possibility of agreement seemed remote. The ZANU group felt that majority rule would only be achieved through armed struggle and their efforts were concentrated into building up a guerrilla force in camps in Tanzania and Zambia. Meanwhile Mozambique continued to allow Rhodesian trade to pass through her ports. By early 1976 the possibility of a Rhodesian settlement had receded considerably. The Victoria Falls Bridge could well remain closed for many more years and the Zambian leaders must feel that they took a wise decision in building a new rail outlet to Dar es Salaam.

After the closure of the Rhodesian border the Benguela railway had become Zambia's main outlet to the sea. By early 1975 it appeared that this line might well prove a more attractive route for Zambia than the Tanzam railway. In October 1974 the £16-million Cubal variant had been opened, elminating a serious bottleneck on the railway, and Portugal's decision to withdraw from Angola, announced in January 1975, meant that the political obstacle to the use of the Benguela line disappeared.

Proposals were then revived for a rail link between the Copperbelt and Angola, by-passing Zaire, in order to provide more direct access to Lobito. This railway, passing through Zambia's North-Western Province, would also serve the Kansanshi copper mine, as well as the Lumwana deposits, and the proposed iron and steel plant to be built near Mwinilunga. In 1975 work began on a feasibility study of this rail project, which would certainly be a competitor to the Tanzam line, but again it is unlikely to be actually built for a number of years.

As Angola's independence date approached, tensions between the three liberation movements increased and ultimately disrupted Zambia's major route to the sea. An interim government of the three movements (MPLA, FNLA, and UNITA) and the Portuguese was formed on 31 January 1975. But all the movements vied with each other for power and the spectre of civil war loomed over the country. Then early in August, just a few weeks before independence, fighting broke out. A FNLA-UNITA coalition soon took over control of the northern and southern parts of the country, while the MPLA retained its hold over the capital of Luanda and the central area of Angola.

Fighting broke out along the Benguela railway and services were halted on 10 August 1975. Part of the line was taken over by UNITA forces, while much of the railway was under MPLA control. Portugal's withdrawal, on 11 November 1975, merely led to an intensification of the civil war, accompanied by greater international intervention. The Soviet Union stepped up its supply of military hardware and advisers to the MPLA. South African troops and the American CIA increased their level of assistance to the FNLA-UNITA coalition. By the time the OAU met in January 1976 independent Africa was completely split over its attitudes to the Angolan war.

Meanwhile Zambia's foreign trade had been completely disrupted by the fighting in Angola, giving the Tanzam outlet a new importance. When the Benguela line was cut in August 1975 more than 100,000 tons of Zambian imports had been dumped on the docks at Lobito. Much of this cargo had to be re-shipped to Dar es Salaam and in September the Tanzam railway was used to carry Zambian imports as far as Kapiri Mposhi for the first time. Three trains a week were used, on an emergency basis, mainly carrying supplies of wheat, timber, and steel into Zambia. The Benguela line was badly damaged during the fighting, so that even after the civil war ended, extensive repairs had to be made to the railway, and it is unlikely that Zambia will be able to use the route during 1976.

When Nyerere and Kaunda decided to accept the Chinese offer to build the Tanzam railway they presumably realized that there was a good chance that by the time the line was completed Rhodesia, Mozambique, and Angola would all be under African rule. There were, however, sufficient reasons for proceeding with the Tanzam project—Zambia's need for an alternative outlet to reduce her dependence on her traditional route and the importance of opening up remote areas of Tanzania and Zambia. If, on the other hand, either Rhodesia, Mozambique, or Angola remained under white rule then it was essential for Zambia to have a rail outlet through independent Africa. Without such a railway the landlocked country would have remained vulnerable to Rhodesian and Portuguese pressure. The Zambian government's decision to proceed with the Tanzam railway was a clear sign of its determination to confront the white South and support the liberation movements in their struggle for majority rule.

# VIII
# FREEDOM RAILWAY

At the very moment when the Tanzam railway was completed it suddenly appeared that the line might become redundant. Dar es Salaam port had been seriously congested and it only had the capacity to handle a small part of Zambia's foreign trade. Increases in harbour charges during 1974 raised fears that the Tanzam route might become more expensive than other outlets. Developments in Southern Africa — particularly the independence of Mozambique and Angola, and the increased likelihood of a Rhodesian settlement — opened up prospects of using the traditional RR route as well as a number of other outlets through the former Portuguese territories. The Tanzam line, its critics gleefully pointed out, would become a ghost line. Nevertheless, 'You can't put all your eggs in one basket', the Zambian Foreign Minister explained, and the country will never again be dependent on a single outlet to the sea.[1] The Tanzam route is still likely to carry the larger part of Zambia's foreign trade.

The international implications of the railway stretch far beyond the borders of the two countries served by the line. The reorientation of Zambia's transport routes played a crucial role in breaking ties with the white South and the forging of new links with the independent states to the north. But in view of the changing situation in Southern Africa, the railway is increasingly being viewed as an important instrument for development, a milestone on the slow and tortuous path towards economic independence.

## HAVEN OF PEACE

As the Tanzam construction teams raced ahead to Kapiri Mposhi, considerably ahead of schedule, a long line of ships queued outside Dar es Salaam harbour waiting to unload. The average waiting time for a berth leapt up to two weeks during 1974, with many vessels having to wait considerably longer. Shipping lines slapped a 30 per cent congestion surcharge—the largest ever imposed at an East African port—on all cargo handled at Dar es Salaam. The harbour, one old expatriate shipping expert complained, was having a severe attack of 'Daressallitis'. By 1975 it appeared that the railway to the Copperbelt would be completed before the Indian Ocean terminal had the capacity to deal with Zambia's trade.

Dar es Salaam—'Haven of Peace' in Arabic—overlooks the coconut-fringed harbour. Two sunken creeks form a protected bay with a narrow entrance channel from the Indian Ocean. A settlement was first established on the bay by the Sultan of Zanzibar in 1862, but it remained little more than a small fishing village until the capital of German East Africa was transfered from Bagamoyo in 1891. During the early years of this century cargo was laboriously manhandled on to lighters and then rolled up the beach. The first wooden jetty was built in 1905 and the completion of the railway to Kigoma, on the eve of World War I, ensured that Dar es Salaam became the country's major port as well as an important outlet for the Belgian territories of Ruanda-Urundi and the eastern Congo.

By 1974 Dar es Salaam harbour was badly congested, queues of ships waited outside the port, the dockside was littered with unidentified cargo, and heavy surcharges were imposed on shipping. This was partly because Lobito—the major port used by Zambia in 1973—was hit by even worse congestion and so during the first half of 1974 Zambia was forced to double its imports sent through Dar es Salaam. At the same time Tanzania had to buy £60 million of food from overseas to cope with a fall in domestic production, largely caused by drought, and imports shot up by over 50 per cent. In addition more than 100,000 tons of construction material were unloaded from Chinese ships for the completion of the Tanzam railway. Dar es Salaam harbour was continuously jammed, with total general cargo imports jumping up a third to reach 1.8 million tons in 1974.

Over the past decade Dar es Salaam port constantly had to cope with considerably larger volumes of traffic than had been anticipated. A massive programme of expansion was undertaken and the number of deep-water berths has been increased from three, at the time of UDI, to eleven. A single-buoy mooring point for oil tankers was opened in 1973, just outside the harbour, which has reduced pressure on port facilities and enabled larger tankers to discharge. There has also been insufficient handling equipment and warehousing space for the volume of cargo passing through the harbour.

Since China was building the railway from Dar es Salaam to the Copperbelt it might have appeared logical for the Chinese to build the necessary berths in the port, and China did, in fact, construct a naval base just opposite the TAZARA docks. Presumably the Tanzanian government was wary of becoming over-dependent on Chinese assistance and there might also have been objections from the other two East African partners in the Harbours Corporation. It was left to the World Bank—which had refused to finance the Tanzam project—to provide the major part of the funds needed to build facilities for handling the railway's cargo.

It was not simply the lack of facilities within the port which slowed down Zambian traffic at Dar es Salaam. Harbour administration has been very poor at times, leading Nyerere to dismiss the Port Manager in November 1974, and dock workers have often been accused of low productivity. An editorial in the *Daily News*, the Tanzanian government newspaper, commented that the main cause of congestion was a mixture of slackness, idleness, indifference and negligence in the port.[2] Documentation problems—due to inefficiency on the part of both the customs department and importers—slowed down clearance of Zambia's imports, and Zambia-Tanzania Road Services have also sometimes been slow to pick up cargo because of a shortage of vehicles.

Tanzanian and Zambian officials have often felt that congestion at Dar es Salaam was highlighted by hostile observers in an attempt to sabotage the Tanzam railway. Nevertheless, the long queues of ships which waited outside the harbour during 1974 made the prospect of using the new railway on an intensive basis rather bleak for the immediate future. Three further berths were commissioned during 1975, but it still appears doubtful whether Dar es Salaam will be able to cope with all the traffic that the railway could generate until the late 1970s.

Critics also maintained that Dar es Salaam port, since it is sited in a confined bay, is too small to be expanded sufficiently to handle the volume of traffic expected after the completion of the new railway. In 1974 a British firm of consultants, Bertlin, produced a report on the development of the harbour. The study recommended, in the light of likely levels of cargo, that two additional berths should be completed by 1980 and suggested that the port would probably then have sufficient capacity until at least 1990.

The Bertlin study also examined the problems involved in developing a port which had two different railway systems, EAR and the Tanzam line, with incompatible gauges. The situation in Dar es Salaam is further complicated because the harbour serves three main hinterlands — Tanzania, and Zambia, as well as Burundi, Rwanda, and Zaire — and one ship often carries cargo for all three areas. Bertlin therefore recommended that goods should be cleared from the harbour by road, rather than directly by rail, with depots established just outside the port area to ease congestion. This proposal was criticized by a Zambian government report, which commented that siting the depots outside the port area would involve unnecessary and costly double-handling of goods.[3] The depots are, however, now under construction.

A further question that remained to be resolved was that of the use of containers. The Zambian government is favourably inclined towards containerization, which is becoming increasingly common in shipping, but there has been some hostility towards this in East Africa. Tanzanian dockworkers have been a strong pressure group rejecting the use of containers, since this would reduce demand for dock labour, and General Amin is believed to have suggested that containers could be used to smuggle in foreign military forces! Rolling stock at present being supplied to TAZARA could not handle containerized cargo.

Not only must sufficient facilities be available for Zambian traffic, if Dar es Salaam is to become Zambia's major outlet, but port charges must also be competitive. On 1 May 1974 new tariffs were introduced in East Africa, involving a massive fourfold increase in charges, which would have cost Zambia an extra £35 million a year. The Zambian government immediately protested against the rise and the two copper companies were apparently requested to re-route exports through other ports. The East African Harbours Corporation argued that its charges had remained substantially the same since 1962 and that they were merely being raised to an economic level. Within a few weeks, however, the East African Communications Council, acting under pressure from Tanzania, offered concessionary rates at Dar es Salaam. These reduced the increases, which still added £4 million to the cost of Zambia's imports and £½ million to exports. Charges at Dar es Salaam were then at a similar level to those at most other Southern African ports.

The tariff issue strengthened Zambia's wish to participate in the East African Harbours Corporation, which would probably involve association with the East African Community, in order to have a degree of direct control over what should become the country's major outlet. The expansion of Dar es Salaam port is 'still shrouded in uncertainty', a Zambian government report pointed out in December 1974,[4] and this has caused a good deal of worry in Lusaka. It is certainly unfortunate that the expansion of the facilities at Dar es Salaam was not begun earlier. But by the late 1970s the situation should be much improved and Dar es Salaam should then be able to cope with the volume of traffic expected after the completion of the new rail link to Zambia.

## FULL STEAM AHEAD

When work began on the Tanzam railway it was envisaged that the new line would carry most of Zambia's foreign trade and in 1973 the Zambian Transport Minister announced that 90 per cent of the country's trade would be routed through Dar es Salaam. Then in 1974 it suddenly appeared that Zambia might well have a choice of possible outlets. With stories of severe congestion and rising port charges at Dar es Salaam, it seemed that the Tanzam railway might become redundant on the very eve of its opening.

The Tanzam line was built to carry up to 2 million tons of traffic a year in each direction. If the number of stations, which provide double-track sections for passing, were increased from 91 to 147, the route would be able to handle 3.5 million tons. The capacity of railway wagons varies considerably, depending on the commodity, but rolling stock for around a million tons will be supplied initially. Presumably, however, additional wagons and locomotives could be obtained. A more serious obstacle is the capacity of Dar es Salaam port. Providing essential improvements are carried out, the Bertlin study estimated that just over 2 million tons of Zambian trade (excluding oil sent by pipeline) could be handled by the 1990s. At present Zambia's general imports amount to about 1½ million tons—the crucial figure, since exports represent only about half that weight. A substantial proportion of this could be railed via Tanzania by the late 1970s, when the Tanzam route is fully operational and Dar es Salaam port's capacity has been increased. The amount that actually goes by this route remains to be determined by the Zambian government.

The Tanzam railway is likely to carry most of Zambia's foreign trade for a number of reasons. First, Zambia is one of the joint owners of TAZARA. The government therefore has a financial stake in the line and would wish to keep TAZARA viable, so that it generates sufficient revenue to meet loan repayments and the operation of the line does not require subsidies from the Treasury. Both Tanzania and Zambia, when they established TAZARA, also undertook to 'make maximum use of the facilities provided by the railway'.[5]

Secondly, the Zambian section of the Tanzam route represents a greater proportion of the distance to the sea than the railways to Beira and Lobito, so that transport charges paid in foreign currency are smaller. On the Tanzam route the total distance that has to be paid for in foreign currency is 583 miles — compared with 958 miles on the line to Beira and 1,464 miles on the Lobito route.

Thirdly, operating costs on the Tanzam railway are likely to be as low as those on the other rail outlets. The total distance to Dar es Salaam, 1,235 miles from Ndola, is shorter than to Beira (by 200 miles) or Lobito (by 239 miles). Gradients on the Tanzam line, on the other hand, are slightly higher than on the other routes and this increases costs. The Anglo-Canadian survey calculated that operating costs on the Tanzam line would be .35 pence per ton-mile, compared with .48 pence on the existing RR route. These figures were, however, based on the assumption that all copper exports and 80 per cent of the Zambia's imports are sent on the Tanzam line. It now appears that a considerably smaller proportion of Zambia's trade will be routed through Dar es Salaam and this is likely to increase costs on the railway.

Tariffs for the Tanzam line have not yet been announced. Zambia, which will be the major user of the railway, will want low tariffs and, because of the existence of a number of alternative routes, the Zambian government will be in a powerful bargaining position. Zambia's copper is a valuable prize for transporters in Central Africa and there will no doubt be competition between the various lines serving the Copperbelt. Indeed this is one of the reasons why the Zambian government wanted an additional outlet to the sea. Since Zambia's trade is imbalanced — with imports weighing twice as much as the country's exports — tariffs on all routes will be partly determined by the degree of balance. Tanzania, which will provide the bulk of the Tanzam railway's agricultural freight, may well press for low rates on these goods in order to encourage development in areas served by the new line.

TAZARA tariffs will, according to the Tanzanian-Zambian agreement which established the organization, be set at levels to break even after operating expenses, repayments to China, and depreciation costs have been paid. Both Tanzania and Zambia, however, have an interest in ensuring that the line attracts sufficient traffic to operate without making a loss, so tariff levels will presumably be competitive with those on alternative routes. Charges at Dar es Salaam, which were raised considerably in 1974, may also influence the volume of Zambian traffic sent on the Tanzam railway. Harbour costs, however, are less than 10 per cent of the rail charges, so they will clearly be a less important consideration.

Finally, Zambia has a strategic interest in making extensive use of the Tanzam railway. Both the other rail routes involve transit through two countries (Rhodesia and Mozambique to Beira, Zaire and Angola to Lobito), with the additional political complications, customs problems, and resulting delays. At least by early 1976 the route through Tanzania appeared the most politically acceptable from the Zambian point of view. The Angolan civil war had closed the Benguela route. It was difficult to predict when a Rhodesian settlement might be reached and what developments there would be in Rhodesia.

The Bertlin study produced estimates of the amount of traffic that the Tanzam railway was likely to carry. It was assumed that Zambian imports would rise by 3 per cent a year (by weight), with copper exports increasing at the slightly lower rate of 2 per cent. The critical assumption was that around 65 per cent of Zambia's foreign trade would be sent through Dar es Salaam. This proportion is likely to fluctuate considerably from year to year, it was admitted, and could be as low as 50 per cent or rise to 80 per cent. In view of the changing political situation in Southern Africa the lower percentage is by far the more likely of the two figures.

The Zambian government can control the amount of traffic passing through Dar es Salaam — both by specifying the route on import licences and by calling for TAZARA to set tariffs at a competitive level — which should ensure that the majority of Zambia's trade goes through Tanzania. Dar es Salaam will be closer to Far Eastern markets, particularly China and Japan, and now that the Suez Canal is open it will also be nearer to European ports. This represents a saving in time and, in some cases, lower costs. Traffic to North America is likely to be routed through Lobito.

Road transport to Dar es Salaam takes three to five days, providing point-to-point delivery, while the rail route will probably take more than ten days. Some imports, particularly perishables, are likely to be sent by Zambia-Tanzania Road Services even after the completion of the Tanzam line. Road charges will be higher than by rail, but the Bertlin study estimated that between 10 per cent and 20 per cent of

Zambian cargo sent through Dar es Salaam would be transported over the Great North Road.

The Tanzam railway, according to the Bertlin survey, is likely to carry 670,000 tons of Zambian imports and 535,000 tons of exports — although these estimates may be on the optimistic side until the late 1970s — and Bertlin suggested that these quantities could rise by 50 per cent to reach 1,044,000 tons of imports and 753,000 tons of exports by the year 1990. Bertlin's figures do not include internal commerce or trade between Tanzania and Zambia. Domestic traffic on the Zambian section of the route is likely to be relatively light, because of the sparsely populated and underdeveloped nature of the Northern Province, but development prospects in Tanzania are much brighter. At least after the mineral deposits in the south-west are opened up there should be considerable internal traffic.

Trade between Zambia and East Africa is still at a relatively low level, although it is growing rapidly. Some commerce between Katanga and Tanzania might be sent over the Tanzam route and it is also possible that some of Katanga's foreign trade, including copper exports, may be railed through Dar es Salaam. The Tanzam railway will almost certainly be the major route for Zambia's foreign trade, although substantial amounts will be sent to outlets in Angola and Mozambique, and increasing amounts of internal traffic and inter-African trade should ensure that the railway to Dar es Salaam operates profitably.

## IMPERIAL DREAM BECOMES PAN-AFRICAN REALITY

Now that the Tanzam line has been completed, only 800 miles of track remains to be laid before the imperial dream becomes reality and Cape Town is linked to Cairo. Ironically it is the Chinese who have done more than anyone during the last 50 years to fulfil the vision of Cecil Rhodes. The role of the Chinese, at least in Western eyes, still remains shrouded in mystery and it is this aspect of the project — rather than the value of the railway to Tanzania and Zambia — which received most comment in the world's press.

For the Chinese the Tanzam railway has been a great success. The generous terms of the loan have been favourably compared with aid provided by the West and the Soviet Union. The modest attitude of the Chinese, from high government officials down to the workers in the bush, made a deep impression on their Tanzanian and Zambian counterparts. The speed with which the railway was completed, more than two years ahead of schedule, as well as the quality of the construction work, are ample testimony to Chinese methods.

The Tanzam railway cemented the growing relationship between China and the two African nations involved in the project. Assistance in building the line increased the level of interaction between the three countries, while the fact that few difficulties arose — and those problems which did emerge normally were quickly resolved — meant that Chinese ties with Dar es Salaam and Lusaka were strengthened.

The implications of the Tanzam railway project, the impact of which was felt far beyond the frontiers of Tanzania and Zambia, affected China's relations with Africa as a whole. During the 1960s there was strong hostility towards the People's Republic, often actively encouraged by the United States, and the announcement of Chinese involvement in the Tanzam railway sparked off criticism in neighbouring countries such as Kenya, the Congo, and Malawi. But by the time the line had been completed China had become a 'respectable' member of the international community and the number of African countries maintaining diplomatic relations with Peking jumped from thirteen in 1967 to thirty by 1974.

Tanzania and Zambia played a role — even if comparatively marginal — in integrating the People's Republic into the international system. Nyerere and Kaunda may well have been consulted by fellow African heads of state on the desirability of developing relations with Peking. The Tanzanian and Zambian leaders, particularly after their extensive contacts with the Chinese over the railway project, would no doubt have encouraged other African governments to establish ties with the People's Republic.

Accounts of China's assistance with the Tanzam railway — and the notable absence of dangers, such as 'subversion', which critics of China had warned about — must have played a part in making Peking's aid more attractive to other African states. President Mobutu, for example, visited the People's Republic in January 1973 and accepted a loan of £50 million. The leader of Zaire, who had previously been very hostile towards China, may well have been influenced by observing Chinese activities in neighbouring Tanzania and Zambia.

A few months later when the Sierra Leonean President arrived in Peking he specifically mentioned the Tanzam project when he thanked the Chinese leaders for the invaluable assistance that they had 'been giving to our brothers and sisters in other parts of the continent of Africa'.[6] The Tanzam railway was a glowing advertisement for Chinese aid and the rapid increase in the number of African states receiving assistance from Peking—which jumped from thirteen in June 1971 to twenty-nine by the end of 1973—could have been at least partly due to the success of the rail project.

The Friendship Route, as the Chinese called the Tanzam railway, was regarded in Peking as an instrument to cement the growing ties with Tanzania and Zambia in order to strengthen these two African states. A stronger Third World would play an important role in reducing the power of China's principal enemies, the two super-powers, so support for Africa fitted in with Peking's global strategy. Tanzania and Zambia never developed extensive ties with the Soviet Union. But the growing friendship with China, and particularly the decision to accept Chinese aid for the Tanzam railway, certainly affected relations with the West.

Tanzanian and Zambian friendship with China had a dual impact on relations with the Western world. The two African states, so Washington believed, had embarked on the slippery path towards communism. On the one hand this encouraged the United States to try to outflank the Chinese and this partly accounted for the extensive assistance provided for the improvement of the Great North Road. Chinese aid for the Tanzam railway—a technologically complex and financially costly project — also altered the perceptions of the Tanzanian and Zambian leaders. It encouraged the two African governments to stand firm against Western pressures and instead pursue more independent policies.

The Tanzanian and Zambian governments were less concerned with the effect of the railway on their relations with aid donors and more interested in the impact of the project on their inter-African relations. Zambia occupies a pivotal role in Africa south of the Equator because of its central geographical position. The country shares borders with no less than eight neighbours—four of them under white rule until 1975—and so the Tanzam railway, since it is part of a fundamental reorientation in Zambia's external relations, will cause major repercussions reaching far beyond the nation's frontiers.

The Tanzam railway was conceived at a time when the Zambezi River was becoming the border between black and white Africa—the Maginot line of Southern Africa—and the route was seen as an important element in Zambia's attempt to escape from dependence on the minority regimes. Only then could the Zambian government risk giving full support to the liberation movements. The wisdom of proceeding with the project was demonstrated in January 1973, with the closure of Zambia's traditional rail outlet over the Victoria Falls Bridge, when the country was able to take the courageous decision to break off most of its remaining ties with Southern Africa.

The border closure, which weakened the minority regimes, played a part in the transformation of the situation in Southern Africa. Mozambique and Angola won their independence from Portuguese colonial rule during 1975. The Rhodesian regime has come under increasing pressure from its neighbours. There is likely to be an independent Zimbabwe by the end of the 1970s. This would presumably lead to a re-opening of Zambia's traditional rail route to Beira and an increase in economic links with Rhodesia. But the Zambian government will no doubt be reluctant to revert to the imbalanced economic relationship that existed with Rhodesia during the colonial period. Zambia, her leaders have stressed, will never again want to remain dependent on a single outlet to the sea.

The Tanzam railway, originally seen by Nyerere and Kaunda as part of the barrier between black and white Africa, may now become a link in the way envisaged by Cecil Rhodes. Already the rail project has brought Tanzania and Zambia closer together. Joint consultations had to be held over sensitive issues, such as contacts with potential foreign donors and over the security measures necessary to protect the line. TAZARA, a joint Tanzanian-Zambian corporation, was established to provide the organizational framework for the project. Finally, improved communications between the two countries should also provide the essential infrastructure for greater economic integration.

Nyerere and Kaunda had become colleagues by the early 1960s and their political outlooks encompassed many common elements. TANU and UNIP have also developed close links and the ideologies of the two governments—Tanzanian *ujamaa* and Zambian Humanism—include many similarities. But until recently Tanzanian-Zambian ties were very largely based on the personal relationship between the two leaders. The alliance, now it has been cemented with more substantive links, is increasingly likely to survive the present occupants of State House in Dar es Salaam and Lusaka.

Some observers have speculated on the possibility of closer political ties between the two countries. This might possibly be on the model of the Tanganyika-Zanzibar union which, despite much talk of Pan-Africanism, has been the only instance of two independent African states successfully giving up their sovereignty to unite. But the creation of a 'Republic of Tanzambia' is remote in the foreseeable future. Different economic and political structures would make unification a slow and complex process. A glance at the attempts at political integration in the rest of Africa is enough to reveal the pitfalls that have to be avoided. What can be predicted, however, is a gradual strengthening of the ties between Tanzania and Zambia with the completion of the new rail link.

Tanzania, some observers have claimed, has already become less interested in her links with East Africa as new ties have been developed with Zambia. The Tanzam railway, far from being an instrument of unity, could well be one of the causes behind the disintegration of East African co-operation. It is true that there has been a serious deterioration in relations between the three East African states since the late 1960s and the continued existence of the East African Community is in jeopardy. But the causes are numerous and the establishment of Tanzanian ties with Zambia had probably only had a very marginal impact.

The Ugandan *coup* ended bilateral relations with Tanzania, bringing the two countries to the brink of war on several occasions, and complicating the operation of the East African Community. Tanzania's relations with Kenya have been strained because of differing economic systems, with Kenya opting for a capitalist development strategy, and the serious deficit which Tanzania suffers on her trade with Kenya. It should be remembered, however, that Tanzania still retains close economic ties with Kenya and that trade between the two countries is still more than ten times the volume that it is with Zambia. Tanzanian links with Zambia, and particularly the decision to proceed with the Tanzam railway, have become a scapegoat to divert attention from the problems within East Africa.

Just as the Tanzam railway will enable Tanzania to look southwards, away from East Africa, so it will also bring Zambia nearer to the rest of East Africa. Zambia already has considerably greater trade with Kenya than with Tanzania, so that some of the benefits of the new railway will certainly accrue to Kenyan exporters. Nyerere has called for an expansion of the East African Community—which might ultimately include Zambia, Zaire, Mozambique, and Malawi—and this could create a strong regional unit tied together by the Tanzam link. But serious problems remain to be resolved before an economic grouping of this size can be created.

Zambia is likely to develop as an important transit centre in

Central Africa. The ZR line already extends into Zaire and the decision has been taken to build a rail link to Malawi. Discussions have also taken place on the construction of railways into Angola and Mozambique and, whether or not they are built, economic links with the former Portuguese territories will certainly be developed. The completion of the BotZam road in 1975 and the prospect of a Rhodesian settlement will improve communications southwards. The Tanzam railway could therefore give East Africa more direct access to the whole of Central Africa and provide an impetus for regional integration.

### ESCAPE ROUTE FROM POVERTY

The Tanzam route not only provides Zambia with an alternative outlet to the sea—which implies that the country must remain dependent on overseas trade—but it should also act as a catalyst in developing the two countries which it serves. Increasingly the Tanzam project is being regarded as more than a strategic asset to free Zambia from dependence on Rhodesia; the line is now seen primarily as an instrument of development. The two aims were, in any case, closely related. 'Our political independence depends upon the degree of our economic independence', Nyerere once remarked, 'as well as the nature of our economic development depending upon our political independence.'[7]

The line passes through regions of great economic potential which have remained unexploited because of the lack of transport facilities. It is still rather early to determine how much development is likely to be stimulated by the new railway—since communications are only one factor, even if an essential one, in the process of development—and it appears that the two governments have been somewhat slow in planning projects along the Tanzam corridor. But just one scheme, the exploitation of mineral deposits in south-west Tanzania, may be an important stage in altering the structure of the country's economy. The railway could be a useful instrument in the attempt to reduce Tanzanian dependence on exports of agricultural commodities and Zambia's reliance on copper.

In addition, the railway should stimulate economic co-operation between the two countries served by the line. Trade in Africa, both domestically and among neighbouring states, has been retarded by the external orientation of African economies. The Tanzam route, even though it links the Copperbelt to the sea, should increase the possibilities for Tanzanian-Zambian economic integration. But again this will not be an automatic process—the economic relationships established during the colonial period have often proved difficult to break—and positive steps will have to be taken by the two governments. Zambia's reorientation away from links with Southern Africa should also facilitate the development of closer ties with Tanzania. Prospects are good, but Tanzanian-Zambian economic integration cannot be achieved overnight.

A final but less tangible result of the construction of the Tanzam railway was the positive impact of Chinese methods and attitudes on the two African countries. These range from the use of labour-intensive techniques on the work site in the bush, right up to the influence of China's experience on Tanzanian and Zambian dignitaries visiting the People's Republic. A new model of development had been opened up, an important alternative to the inherited concepts from the colonial period. Nyerere, on his last trip to Peking, mentioned that there were two things which convinced him that socialism was not a Utopian vision: first, 'Capitalism is ultimately incompatible with the real independence of African states. The second thing which encourages me is China . . . . China is providing an encouragement and an inspiration for younger and smaller nations which seek to build socialist societies.'[8]

Development, as Nyerere caustically put it, must not just be for impressing visiting presidents. The Tanzam railway is certainly impressive. But the project will only benefit a minority of the population unless positive measures are taken. Large schemes of this sort so often lead to the establishment of islands of development—whether it is a mining centre, an industrial plant, or a capital-intensive agricultural project—which bring wealth to the few.

The road from underdevelopment is not an easy one. Most development projects are only partially successful in achieving the aims which had been hoped for by the planners—because of the all-encompassing nature of the process of development—so it would be naïve to expect the Tanzam railway automatically to lead to major changes to the Tanzanian and Zambian economies. All it does is to enlarge the range of options that are open and as such it is an important step towards a more meaningful form of independence for for the two countries served by the line. 'The Tanzam railway is a freedom railway—a railway for African unity and development,' Kaunda proclaimed, but how the route is used will depend on the governments and peoples of Tanzania and Zambia.[9]

# NOTES

## CHAPTER I

1. Quoted in Kasuka Mutukwa, *The International Implications of the Tanzania-Zambia Railway Project* (MA thesis, George Washington University, June 1971), p. 2.
2. Preface to E. Grogan and A. Strong, *From Cape to Cairo* (London, 1900), p. viii.
3. Ibid.
4. Quoted in B. Williams, *Rhodes* (London, 1921), p. 309.
5. Quoted in Mark Strage, *Cape to Cairo* (London, 1973), p. 111.
6. Quoted in James D. Graham, 'The Tanzam Railway', *Africa Today*, Summer 1974, p. 38.
7. *Report of the East Africa Commission* (London, 1925), p. 121.
8. C. Gillman, *Report on the Preliminary Surveys for a Railway Line to Open Up the South West of Tanganyika Territory* (London, 1929), p. 65.
9. *Report on an Engineering Survey of a Rail Link Between the East African and Rhodesian Railway Systems* (Nairobi, 1952), p. 91.
10. *Report on Central African Rail Link Development Survey* (London, 1952), vol. i, p. 2.
11. Ibid., p. 30.
12. C. W. Hobley in Leo Weinthal (Ed.), *The Story of the Cape to Cairo Railway and River Route from 1887 to 1922* (London, 1923), vol. iii, p. 9.
13. Frantz Fanon, *The Wretched of the Earth* (New York, 1968), p. 159.

## CHAPTER II

1. Quoted in Colin Legum (Ed.), *Zambia: Independence and Beyond* (London, 1966), p. 141.
2. Speech of 27 August 1973.
3. Quoted in Strage, op. cit., p. 108.
4. Quoted in Fergus Macpherson, *Kenneth Kaunda of Zambia* (Lusaka, 1974), p. 445.
5. Edwin T. Haefele and Eleanor B. Steinberg, *Government Controls on Transport: An African Case* (Washington, 1965), p. 38.
6. Robert C. Good, *U.D.I.: The International Politics of the Rhodesian Rebellion* (London, 1973), p. 86.
7. Quoted ibid., p. 16.
8. Quoted ibid., p. 121.
9. Quoted in Richard Hall, *The High Price of Principles*

(Harmondsworth, 1973), p. 168.
10. Agreement of 10 December 1963, section 5.
11. *Tanganyika Concessions Limited Report and Accounts 31 July 1967* (London, 1967), p. 6.
12. Quoted in Hall, op. cit., pp. 147-8.
13. *Daily News* (Dar es Salaam), 17 March 1973.


## CHAPTER III

1. *African Development,* June 1973, p. 9.
2. Speech of 28 October 1970.
3. *The Northern Rhodesia-Tanganyika Rail Link* (Washington, 1964), p. i.
4. *Tanganyika-Zambia Highway Study* (Stanford Research Institute, 1966), p. 8.
5. *Report of the UN/ECA/FAO Economic Survey Mission on the Economic Development of Zambia* (Ndola, 1964), p. 127.
6. Haefele and Steinberg, op. cit., p. 56.
7. Quoted in William Edgett Smith, *We Must Run While They Walk* (New York, 1971), p. 229.
8. Ibid., p. 228.
9. *British-Canadian Report on an Engineering and Economic Feasibility Study of a Proposed Zambia-East Africa Rail Link* (London, 1966), p. 11.
10. Ibid., p. 282.
11. Ibid., p. 11.
12. Quoted in Mutukwa, op. cit., p. 25.
13. Quoted in Hall, op. cit., p. 159.
14. Government memorandum, August 1964.
15. Quoted in James C. Curran *Communist China in Black Africa: The Tan-Zam Railway 1965-70* (Carlisle Barracks, 1971), p. 60.
16. Quoted ibid., p. 62.
17. *Africa,* No. 3 (1971), p. 49.
18. Speech of 24 March 1974.
19. Speech of 28 May 1969.
20. *Tanganyika Concessions Limited Report and Accounts 31 July 1970* (London, 1970), p. 24.
21. *Northern Rhodesia-Tanganyika Rail Link,* p. i.


## CHAPTER IV

1. New China News Agency release, 27 December 1961.
2. H. B. Thom (Ed.), *Journal of Jan Van Riebeeck: vol. i, 1651-55* (Cape Town, 1952), p. 33.

3.  *South Africa 1974* (Johannesburg, 1974), p. 930.
4.  *Usambara Post,* 2 June 1906.
5.  Speech of 18 February 1965.
6.  *The Times,* 1 September 1964.
7.  *Guardian,* 3 July 1965.
8.  Quoted in Hall, op. cit., pp. 248-9.
9.  Interview with Vernon Mwaanga, Foreign Minister, Lusaka, October 1974.
10. Speech of 18 February 1965.
11. E. L. Wheelwright and Bruce McFarlane, *The Chinese Road to Socialism* (Harmondsworth, 1973), p. 184.
12. Interview with Li Chiang-fen, Chinese ambassador in Lusaka, October 1974.
13. Interview with senior Chinese official dealing with foreign affairs, Peking, August 1973.
14. Quoted in Bob Hitchcock, *Bwana—Go Home* (London, 1974), p. 54.
15. Teobaldo Filesi, *China and Africa in the Middle Ages* (London, 1972), pp. 2-3.
16. New China News Agency release, 27 October 1970.
17. Alan Hutchison, *China's African Revolution* (London, 1975), p. 278.
18. *Wall Street Journal,* 29 September 1967.
19. Speech of 23 June 1965.
20. *Peking Review,* 5 April 1974.
21. Quoted in *The Times,* 26 October 1970.
22. Speech of 4 June 1965.
23. *Africa,* No. 3 (1971), p. 49.
24. *Daily Express,* 8 September 1965.
25. Hedley A. Chilvers, *The Yellow Man Looks On: Being the Story of the Anglo-Dutch Conflict in Southern Africa and its Interest for the Peoples of Asia* (London, 1933), p. 231.
26. *East African Standard,* 11 October 1970.
27. UN Document A/AC.159/1, 3 May 1974.
28. Curran, op. cit., p. 18.
29. Quoted in Smith, op. cit., p. 234.
30. Quoted in *The Times,* 26 October 1970.
31. *The Second Scramble* (Dar es Salaam, 1961).
32. Speech of 28 October 1970.
33. Quoted in Smith, op. cit., p. 190.
34. Speech of 28 October 1970.
35. Quoted in Colin Legum, 'Africa and China: Symbolism and Substance', in A. M. Halpern (Ed.), *Politics Towards China: Views from Six Continents* (New York, 1965), p. 390.
36. Speech of 21 June 1968.
37. *Daily Mail* (Lusaka), 2 May 1972.
38. Curran, op. cit., p. 42.

## CHAPTER V

1. *Guardian,* 7 October 1972.
2. Major E. S. Grogan in Weinthal, op. cit., p. 13.
3. New China News Agency release, 27 October 1970.
4. *The Sunday Times,* 1 September 1974.
5. *British Canadian Report,* p. 12.
6. Speech of 24 March 1974.
7. Curran, op. cit., p. 67.
8. *New Internationalist,* May 1973, p. 14.
9. *Peking Review,* 4 October 1974, p. 17.
10. *Daily Mail* (Lusaka), 12 September 1973.
11. Speech of 24 March 1974.
12. Quoted in Smith, op. cit., p. 223.
13. *Annual Plan 1970-71* (Dar es Salaam, 1970), p. 53.
14. *Daily Mail* (Lusaka), 30 May 1973.
15. *The Internationalist,* March 1972, p. 13.
16. *The Observer,* 18 February 1973.
17. *The Standard* (Dar es Salaam), 30 March 1972.
18. *New Internationalist,* May 1973, p. 14.
19. *Times of Zambia* (Ndola), 14 March 1971.
20. Interview with Li Chiang-fen, Lusaka, October 1974.
21. *Guardian,* 15 August 1973.
22. Speech of 24 March 1974.
23. *Africa,* May 1974, p. 17.
24. *Z Magazine,* October 1973, pp. 30-1.
25. *The Nation* (Nairobi), 2 February 1969.
26. *Afro-Asian Solidarity Against Imperialism* (Peking, 1964), pp. 149-50.
27. Interview with senior official in Peking, August 1973.


## CHAPTER VI

1. *Enterprise,* No. 3 (1974), p. 4.
2. Quoted in Graham, op. cit., p. 40.
3. *British-Canadian Report,* p. 2.
4. Speech of 28 October 1970.
5. *The Financial Times,* 9 December 1971.
6. National Assembly, 18 January 1974.

## CHAPTER VII

1. Speech of 19 May 1971.
2. Quoted in *Zambia 1964-74* (Lusaka, 1974), p. 9.
3. Quoted in Hutchison, op. cit., p. 228.
4. *Daily News* (Dar es Salaam), 24 June 1973.
5. Speech of 28 October 1970.
6. *Guardian,* 10 January 1973.
7. Quoted in *The Rhodesia-Zambia Border Closure* (London, 1973), p. 8.
8. *The Times,* 5 February 1973.
9. *The Times,* 6 February 1973.
10. *Observer,* 21 January 1973.
11. Ibid.


## CHAPTER VIII

1. Interview with Vernon Mwaanga, Lusaka, October 1974.
2. *Daily News* (Dar es Salaam), 19 November 1974.
3. *Mid-Term Review of the Second National Development Plan* (Lusaka, 1974), p. 87.
4. Ibid.
5. *TAZARA Act,* Article xi.
6. *Peking Review.*
7. Speech of 13 April 1970.
8. Speech of 24 March 1974.
9. Speech of 27 August 1973.

# APPENDIX

## EIGHT PRINCIPLES OF CHINESE AID

*The Eight Principles of Chinese Aid announced by Chou En-lai at Accra on 15 January 1964:*

In providing economic and technical aid to other countries, the Chinese government strictly observes the following eight principles:

*First,* the Chinese government always bases itself on the principle of equality and mutual benefit in providing aid to other countries. It never regards such aid as a kind of unilateral alms but as something mutual. Through such aid the friendly new emerging countries gradually develop their own national economy, free themselves from colonial control and strengthen the anti-imperialist forces in the world. This is in itself a tremendous support to China.

*Second,* in providing aid to other countries, the Chinese government strictly respects the sovereignty of the recipient countries, and never asks for any privileges or attaches any conditions.

*Third,* the Chinese government provides economic aid in the form of interest-free or low-interest loans and extends the time limit for the repayment so as to lighten the burden of the recipient countries as far as possible.

*Fourth,* in providing aid to other countries, the purpose of the Chinese government is not to make the recipient countries dependent on China but to help them embark on the road of self-reliance step by step.

*Fifth,* the Chinese government tries its best to help the recipient countries build projects which require less investment while yielding quicker results, so that the recipient governments may increase their income and accumulate capital.

*Sixth,* the Chinese government provides the best-quality equipment and material of its own manufacture at international market prices. If the equipment and material provided by the Chinese government are not up to the agreed specifications and quality, the Chinese government undertakes to replace them.

*Seventh,* in giving any particular technical assistance, the Chinese government will see to it that the personnel of the recipient country fully master such technique.

*Eighth,* the experts dispatched by the Chinese government to help in construction in the recipient countries will have the same standard of living as the experts of the recipient country. The Chinese experts are not allowed to make any special demands or enjoy any special amenities.

# SELECT BIBLIOGRAPHY

BALLANCE, Frank C., *Zambia and the East African Community* (Syracuse: Program of Eastern African Studies, 1971).

BARTKE, Wolfgang, *China's Economic Aid* (London, 1975).

BOSTOCK, R. M., 'The Transport Sector', in Charles Elliott (Ed.), *Constraints on the Economic Development of Zambia* (Nairobi, 1971), pp. 323-76.

'China and the Tazara Railroad Project', *Current Scene*, May-June 1975, pp. 14-21.

CROXTON, Anthony H., *Railways of Rhodesia* (Newton Abbott, 1973).

CURRAN, James C., *Communist China in Black Africa: The Tan-Zam Railway, 1965-70* (Carlisle Barracks, Pa.: Army War College, 1971).

GRAHAM, James D., 'The Tanzam Railway', *Africa Today*, Summer 1974, pp. 27-42.

DOGANIS, R. S., 'Zambia's Outlet to the Sea: A Case Study in Colonial Transport Development', *Journal of Transport Economics and Policy*, January 1967, pp. 46-51.

GOOD, Robert C., *U.D.I.: The International Politics of the Rhodesian Rebellion* (London, 1973).

GRUNDY, Kenneth W., *Confrontation and Accommodation in Southern Africa: The Limits of Independence* (Berkeley, 1973).

HAEFELE, Edwin T. and Steinberg, Eleanor B., *Government Controls on Transport: An African Case* (Washington, 1965).

HALL, Richard, *The High Price of Principles* (Harmondsworth, 1973).

HILL, Mervyn F., *Permanent Way*, Vol. ii The Story of Tanganyika Railways (Nairobi, 1957).

HUTCHISON, Alan, *China's African Revolution* (London, 1975).

LARKIN, Bruce D., *China and Africa 1949-1970* (Berkeley, 1971).

MAKONI, Tonderai, 'The Economic Appraisal of the Tanzania-Zambia Railway', *African Review*, Vol. ii No. 4, pp. 595-616.

MIHALYI, L. J., 'Some Socio-Economic Projections of the New Line-of-rail in the Geography of Zambia', *East African Universities Social Science Council Conference*, December 1972, paper no. 48.

MUTUKWA, Kasuka, *The International Implications of the Tanzania-Zambia Railway Project* (MA thesis, George Washington University, June 1971).

OGUNSANWO, Alaba, *China's Policy in Africa 1958-71* (London, 1974).

OSTRANDER, F. Taylor, 'Zambia in the Aftermath of Rhodesian UDI: Logistical and Economic Problems', *African Forum*, Winter 1967, pp. 50-65.

*Report on an Engineering Survey of a Rail Link between the East African and Rhodesian Railway Systems* (Nairobi: East African Railways and Harbours Administration, 1952).

*Report on Central African Rail Link Development Survey* (London: Gibb & Partners, 1952), 2 vols.

SKLAR, Richard L., 'Zambia's Response to the Rhodesian Unilateral Declaration of Independence', in William Tordoff, *Politics in Zambia* (Manchester, 1975), pp. 320-62.

SMITH, William Edgett, *We Must Run While They Walk* (New York, 1971).

'The Tanzam Railway', *Jenga*, No. 11, pp. 21-7.

WEINTHAL, Leo (Ed.), *The Story of the Cape to Cairo Railway and River Route from 1881 to 1922* (London, 1923), 4 vols.

WOLFE, Alvin W., 'Tanzania-Zambia Railway: Escape Route from Neocolonial Control?', in A. Carvely (Ed.), *Nonaligned Third World Annual 1970* (St Louis, 1970), pp. 92-103.

*World Bank Mission's Report on the North East Rail Link* (Lusaka: Ministry of Transport and Works, 1964).

YU, George T., *China and Tanzania: A Study in Comparative Interaction* (Berkeley, 1970).

YU, George T., 'Working on the Railroad:·China and the Tanzania-Zambia Railway' *Asian Survey*, November 1971, pp. 1101-17.

*Z Magazine*, May 1973 (pp. 4-7 and 22), October 1973 (pp. 16-21), and November 1975 (pp. 4-7 and 11).

# INDEX

with China, 73, 150; with Zambia, 29-30, 149

Zambia, 128; original rail network, 1-6; rail outlet through Rhodesia, 21-5, 131-2; rail outlet to Angola, 28-31, 132-4; rail outlet through Zaire, 31-2; relations with Britain, 49, 67; with China, 62-3, 66, 82; with East Africa, 121-2, 145, 153; with Mozambique, 26; with Rhodesia, 20, 131-2; with South Africa, 20, 27, 128; with Soviet Union, 67-8; with Tanzania, 16-17, 119-24, 152-3; with Zaire, 29-30, 149; agricultural development along Tanzam route, 17-18, 109-12; role of copper in economy, 109-10

Zambia Air Cargoes, 33

Zambia-East Africa Inter-Governmental Ministerial Committee, 41, 50, 52

Zambia Railways, 25-6, 47, 51, 96, 129, 134

Zambia-Tanzania Road Services, 35, 144

ZANU (Zimbabwe African National Union), 139

Zanzibar, 45-6, 60, 68, 73, 75-8

ZAPU (Zimbabwe African People's Union), 139